speakout **2ND** EDITION

Intermediate
Workbook

with key

Antonia Clare • JJ Wilson
Stephanie Dimond-Bayir

CONTENTS

1 IDENTITY — Page 4

1.1
VOCABULARY | language
GRAMMAR | question forms
LISTENING | leaning languages
WRITING | emails of introduction; learn to write formal and informal emails

1.2
VOCABULARY | relationships
GRAMMAR | review of verb tenses
READING | Men and women – what they say about each other
VOCABULARY PLUS | collocations

1.3
VOCABULARY | interview advice
FUNCTION | talking about yourself
LEARN TO | use two-word responses

2 TALES — Page 9

2.1
VOCABULARY | types of story
GRAMMAR | present perfect and past simple
VOCABULARY PLUS | prepositions
READING | Forever young: James Dean

2.2
LISTENING | Flashbulb memories
GRAMMAR | narrative tenses
VOCABULARY | the news
WRITING | a news report; learn to use time linkers

2.3
VOCABULARY | say/tell
FUNCTION | telling a story
LEARN TO | show interest

Review 1 — Page 14

3 FUTURE — Page 18

3.1
VOCABULARY | organisation
LISTENING | What are your plans?
GRAMMAR | the future (plans)
WRITING | messages; learn to use note form

3.2
READING | Science in the future: discoveries
VOCABULARY | future time markers
GRAMMAR | the future (predictions)
VOCABULARY PLUS | idioms

3.3
FUNCTION | dealing with misunderstandings
LEARN TO | reformulate

4 JOBS — Page 23

4.1
VOCABULARY | personal qualities
GRAMMAR | must/have to/should (obligation)
LISTENING | talking about jobs
VOCABULARY PLUS | confusing words

4.2
READING | Dream job turns into nightmare
VOCABULARY | extreme adjectives
GRAMMAR | used to, would
WRITING | a covering letter; learn to organise your ideas

4.3
VOCABULARY | business
FUNCTION | reaching agreement
LEARN TO | manage a discussion

Review 2 — Page 28

5 SOLUTIONS — Page 32

5.1
LISTENING | talking about changes
GRAMMAR | comparatives and superlatives
VOCABULARY | technology
WRITING | an advantages/disadvantages essay; learn to use discourse markers

5.2
VOCABULARY | information
GRAMMAR | question tags
READING | I never knew that!
VOCABULARY PLUS | word building: adjectives

5.3
VOCABULARY | problems and solutions
FUNCTION | polite requests
LEARN TO | respond to requests

6 EMOTION — Page 37

6.1
VOCABULARY | -ing/-ed adjectives
READING | Stressed out? Take control.
GRAMMAR | real conditionals
VOCABULARY PLUS | multi-word verbs

6.2
VOCABULARY | verb–noun collocations
GRAMMAR | hypothetical conditional: present/future
LISTENING | Who is a potential victim?
WRITING | an email of advice; learn to qualify what you say

6.3
VOCABULARY | life events
FUNCTION | giving news
LEARN TO | respond to news

Review 3 — Page 42

CONTENTS

7 SUCCESS — Page 46

7.1
VOCABULARY | success
READING | Making it happen
GRAMMAR | present perfect simple versus continuous
VOCABULARY *PLUS* | verb phrases

7.2
VOCABULARY | ability
GRAMMAR | present and past ability
LISTENING | William Sidis – life of a genius
WRITING | a summary; learn to make notes for a summary

7.3
VOCABULARY | qualifications
FUNCTION | clarifying opinions

8 COMMUNITIES — Page 51

8.1
VOCABULARY | getting on
GRAMMAR | articles and quantifiers
LISTENING | Who are your neighbours?
VOCABULARY *PLUS* | compound nouns

8.2
VOCABULARY | the internet
GRAMMAR | relative clauses
READING | Silver surfers
WRITING | a website review; learn to use complex sentences

8.3
VOCABULARY | welcoming
FUNCTION | being a good guest
LEARN TO | accept apologies

Review 4 — Page 56

9 HISTORY — Page 60

9.1
VOCABULARY | history
GRAMMAR | hypothetical conditional: past
LISTENING | Fascinating facts – inventions
WRITING | a short essay; learn to structure paragraphs

9.2
GRAMMAR | active versus passive
VOCABULARY | periods of time
VOCABULARY *PLUS* | collocations
READING | Generations and generalisations

9.3
VOCABULARY | describing people
FUNCTION | expressing uncertainty
LEARN TO | react to information

10 WORLD — Page 65

10.1
VOCABULARY | the environment
LISTENING | Earth Hour
GRAMMAR | reported speech
VOCABULARY *PLUS* | word building: prefixes

10.2
VOCABULARY | reporting verbs
READING | A taste of your life
GRAMMAR | verb patterns
WRITING | a restaurant review; learn to link ideas

10.3
VOCABULARY | airports
FUNCTION | giving advice/warnings
LEARN TO | make generalisations

Review 5 — Page 70

AUDIO SCRIPTS — Page 74

ANSWER KEY — Page 82

IDENTITY 1

VOCABULARY
LANGUAGE

1 A Read the information about Shin. Rearrange the letters in italics to complete the sentences.

1 My family is British Chinese so I grew up *uginblial*, speaking Chinese and English. ___bilingual___
2 Actually, I have a high level of *yucenfl* in Spanish, too. _____
3 Of course, many of my friends are British so their *rethom goetun* is English. _____
4 However London is very cosmopolitan – it is easy to meet *ginerof* people here. _____
5 My best friend Sylvie is from Poland but she sounds like a *vetina preeska*. _____
6 Sometimes I teach her *glans* as she didn't learn informal words in school. _____
7 And she teaches me computer *gronja* – I find it difficult but she works in IT! _____
8 In some ways Sylvie has better *gleranin stetsgerai* than me. _____
9 I think her strongest *kills* is writing – she is amazing. _____
10 I am quite careless in comparison and my *cccaaury* can be weak. _____

B Use the words from Exercise 1A to complete the sentences. You may need to change the form of the word.

1 ___Bilingualism___ is an advantage in today's world.
2 My mother is _____ in several languages – she's really clever.
3 I wish I could use language more _____. I make a lot of mistakes.
4 What is your _____? You sound German.
5 He always feels like a _____ in his own country because he hasn't lived there for years.
6 I don't like _____; I prefer it when people use standard English.
7 Do you have good listening _____?
8 Dan is a _____ so he checks all the English in the business documents.

Good morning!

Buenos días!

GRAMMAR
QUESTION FORMS

2 A Circle the question with the correct form.

1 a) What kind of activity you helps learn new vocabulary?
  b) What kind of activity helps you learn new vocabulary?
2 a) Which language you wanted to learn when you were younger?
  b) Which language did you want to learn when you were younger?
3 a) You ever wish you had a different mother tongue?
  b) Do you ever wish you had a different mother tongue?
4 a) What type of thing you do read in English?
  b) What type of thing do you read in English?
5 a) As a child, did you like finding out about different countries?
  b) As a child, did you to like finding out about different countries?
6 a) When did you first speak to a foreign person?
  b) When you first speak to a foreign person?
7 a) If you have to speak in English, what do you always worry?
  b) If you have to speak in English, what do you always worry about?

B Match questions 1–7 in Exercise 2A with answers a)–g).

a) Oh, English of course because it is international. *2*
b) Yes. I was always interested in different cultures.
c) Mostly my pronunciation – I don't feel confident about it.
d) I review a few words every day and write example sentences.
e) A few years ago on my first trip abroad.
f) Not really. But I wish I had learnt English earlier.
g) Websites mostly, for online news. And sometimes magazines about films.

3 A ▷ 1.1 Listen and write the questions you hear.
1 _____
2 _____
3 _____
4 _____
5 _____
6 _____

B Listen again and repeat, paying attention to the intonation.

LISTENING

4 A ▶ 1.2 **Listen to three people answering the questions below. Write their answers.**

Which language did you learn?
How did you learn it?

	Which?	How?
Maria	_____	_____
Ahmed	_____	_____
Jessie	_____	_____

B Listen again and answer the questions.

1 Which country outside Europe did Maria visit?

_____

2 What is her job now?

_____

3 Where did Ahmed move to?

_____

4 How did he communicate to start with?

_____

5 Why does Jessie think British people don't learn other languages?

_____

6 Which country did she live in for a while?

_____

C Read the extracts from the recording. What do you think the words and phrases in bold mean? Match them with meanings a)–f).

1 … they were really **keen** for me to learn English …
2 It was a **culture shock** …
3 … living in Beirut always felt very **cosmopolitan**.
4 But I did some **part-time** Dutch lessons …
5 … we aren't **brilliant** at learning new languages.
6 I **picked** it **up** in my day-to-day life.

a) a feeling of confusion when in a new and different country
b) extremely intelligent or skilled
c) for only part of a day or a week
d) very interested, wanting to do something very much
e) to learn informally without lessons by exposure
f) having people from different parts of the world

WRITING

EMAILS OF INTRODUCTION; LEARN TO WRITE FORMAL AND INFORMAL EMAILS

5 A Read the purposes of two emails. Which email needs to be formal?

1 Introduce myself to a member of my host family in Spain before I visit.
2 Introduce myself as the new chairperson of the Teachers' Association.

B Read the emails and underline the correct alternatives.

To: psanchez@yoohoo.es
Subject: hi!
From: danielagjones@hitmail.com
[1]*Hi Pilar/Dear Madam Pilar*,
[2]*I am writing to greet you./How are you?* As you know, I'm going to stay with you this summer. I [3]*have decided to/thought I'd* send an email to introduce myself. My name's Daniela, but my friends call me Danny, and I hope you will, too.
I'm eighteen years old and at university here in Manchester, studying Business and Economics. I've got lots of hobbies. I love horse-riding, swimming, listening to music, and I also play the flute. My favourite hobby, though, is dancing. I [4]*am particularly keen on/really like* samba and salsa.
I [5]*can't wait to stay/look forward to staying* with you in Spain, though my Spanish isn't very good!
[6]*Hope/I do hope* to hear from you soon.
Danny

To: membership@taas.com
Subject: Introductions
From: hatquistj@ltsu.edu
[7]*Dear members/Hello everybody*,
[8]*I'm writing to say hi/I am writing to introduce myself.* As many of you know, I will begin in the role of chairperson of the Teachers' Association of Amlen State at the end of this month. [9]*I would like to take this opportunity/I really want* to outline my major plans for the Association over the coming year.
I am a maths and physics teacher. I have been in the profession for over forty years in a variety of roles: teacher, administrative assistant, head teacher and school inspector.
My first priority is to increase membership. In the last six years we have seen a decrease of almost 30% in our numbers. I have various proposals for achieving this, which [10]*I'll tell you about/I will explain* during our first meeting next month.
[11]*I look forward to working with you all/See you all soon.*
[12]*All the best/Yours sincerely*,
Jacqueline Hatquist

C Read the instructions and write an email (120–150 words).

You are going on an adventure trip for students of English. You will join ten other students from all over the world on a one-month tour of India. The tour will include cultural visits and two hours of English lessons every day. Write an email of introduction to the other students.

VOCABULARY

RELATIONSHIPS

1 A Put the words in the box into categories 1–4.

employee   fiancée   fiancé   classmate   pupil   boss
team-mate   godfather   godmother   member

1 Person you work with:

_____

2 Person who studies with you:

_____

3 Person you are close to (almost family):

_____

4 Person you do a hobby with:

_____

B Complete the sentences with the words in Exercise 1A.

1 This is Marianna, my _____. We're getting married next year.

2 Dave is my _____. We're both in Year 12 at Cokethorpe High School.

3 She asked her _____ for some time off work, but he said no.

4 I'm a _____ of a swimming club. We meet twice a week at the sports centre.

5 Luisa got 100% in her exam. She's the best _____ in my class.

6 He's an _____ of GEO Foods. He's been there for six years.

7 When I was born, my father asked John, his best friend, to be my _____.

8 Leticia is my _____. We play in the same basketball team.

2 A Underline the stressed syllable in the words in italics.

1 He was an *employee* here.

2 I had a wonderful *mentor*.

3 All *pupils* wear a uniform.

4 We were *team-mates* for years.

5 Have you met my *fiancée*?

6 Talk to your *partner*.

7 She's my *godmother*.

8 That club is for *members* only.

B ▶ 1.3 Listen and check. Then listen and shadow the sentences (say them at the same time).

GRAMMAR

REVIEW OF VERB TENSES

3 Complete the conversations with the correct form of the verbs in brackets.

1 A: I need a holiday, but flights _____ (be) always expensive at this time of year.
B: That's true, but I _____ (find) a cheap flight to Mexico on the net yesterday.

2 A: Grace _____ (win) the lottery last week!
B: That's right. She _____ (sleep) when her brother called to tell her.

3 A: I _____ (not like) football.
B: Why _____ you _____ (not tell) me earlier? The tickets cost £70 each!

4 A: _____ you _____ (hear) about the accident last week?
B: Yes, the boys _____ (drive) along Court Street when a motorbike hit the car.

5 A: _____ you _____ (need) somewhere to stay? I have a spare room.
B: No, it's OK. I _____ (stay) with my sister.

6 A: I _____ (read) a novel called *The Luminaries* at the moment.
B: Oh yes. I found it so boring that I _____ (not finish) it.

7 A: I like an early start, so I _____ (get up) at six every morning.
B: Me too. I always _____ (leave) the house by seven.

8 A: John! Are you ready? We _____ (wait) for you!
B: OK, here I am! Sorry about that. I _____ (look) for my hat! I couldn't find it anywhere.

4 Match beginnings a) and b) with endings i) and ii).

1 a) Do you use the computer? *ii*
  b) Are you using the computer? *i*
  i) I need it for a few minutes.
  ii) Or is everything done by phone?

2 a) She tries to work
  b) She's trying to work
  i) , so please be quiet.
  ii) on her book for two hours every day.

3 a) It doesn't snow
  b) It isn't snowing,
  i) much in New Mexico.
  ii) so we can go out now.

4 a) What are you doing
  b) What do you do
  i) for a living?
  ii) now? Do you want to go for a coffee?

5 a) He was playing squash
  b) He played squash
  i) for the team last year.
  ii) when he broke his ankle.

READING

5 A Do you think statements 1–4 are about men or women? Who said them: men or women?

1 They do things first, and think about the risks later.
2 They remember useless information.
3 They notice when something is dirty or needs replacing.
4 They always remember birthdays and anniversaries.

B Read the text below and check.

C Write the name of the person who makes similar statements to the ones below.

1 Men hate to say, 'I don't know'. ____Aisha____
2 Men cannot 'multitask'; they can only concentrate on one thing at a time. _____
3 Men are very direct when they need something. _____
4 Women are more fluent than men when they speak. _____
5 Women are more maternal; they understand what is good for young children. _____
6 Women have better memories for dates than men. _____

D Find words in the text to match definitions 1–5.

1 the ability to see the position, size or shape of things (paragraph 2) _____
2 give you the tools or abilities that you need (paragraph 2) _____
3 more or to a greater degree (paragraph 3) _____
4 not closely (paragraph 5) _____
5 natural abilities or feelings that make people and animals know something (paragraph 7) _____

VOCABULARY PLUS

COLLOCATIONS

6 Complete the phrases with *go*, *take*, *get* or *do*. Use each verb three times.

1 _get_ a job
2 _____ off coffee
3 _____ part in a quiz
4 _____ some research
5 _____ my homework
6 _____ on with people
7 _____ grey
8 _____ her a favour
9 _____ responsibility
10 _____ angry
11 _____ up the guitar
12 _____ for a walk

---

chatzone 1

Men and Women – What They Say About Each Other

1 The battle of the sexes has probably been going on since the first caveman left his dirty dishes on the floor of the cave. A subject of endless discussion, it has inspired a million jokes and articles and almost as many books.

2 However, a recent study tells us that men and women really do think differently. Our brains are built in a different way. The results of the study suggest that men have better spatial perception (driving, ball sports), while women's brains equip them better for remembering words and speaking fluently.

3 The scientists examined only a small part of the brain, and they say that further research needs to be done. Here at *chatzone1* we have done some less scientific research. We asked people, 'What are the differences between the sexes?' Here are their answers.

What women say about men

4 Men remember useless information, like how fast an aeroplane can go, even if they'll never fly one. (Heather)

If you ask a man a question, he'll always have an answer, even if it's the wrong one. (Aisha)

Men do things first, and think about the risks later. (Candy)

Men cannot watch sport on TV and talk to women at the same time. (Mai)

What men say about men

5 Men know that common house spiders aren't as dangerous as rattlesnakes. (Daniel)

Men can drive without looking at themselves in the mirror every ten seconds. (Ron)

Men can watch a whole film without interrupting to ask, 'Who is he?' 'What's her job?' 'Does he like her?' (Alfred)

When men want something, they ask for it instead of making a comment distantly related to the subject and hoping their partner will guess what the real subject is. (Guy)

What men say about women

6 Women couldn't invent weapons that kill, only weapons that make you feel really guilty until you say sorry. (Kent)

While men speak in sentences, women speak in paragraphs. (Sergio)

Women are happy to own twenty CDs, while men need 200. (Steve)

Women order salad, then eat the man's chips. (Kazeem)

What women say about women

7 Women have natural instincts about what is dangerous for babies. (Linda)

Women notice when something is dirty or needs replacing. (Carol)

Only women can understand other women. (Xun)

Women have a calendar in their brains: we remember birthdays and anniversaries easily. (Avril)

VOCABULARY
INTERVIEW ADVICE

1 Match 1–8 with a)–h) to make advice.

1 Don't avoid eye
2 The most important thing is to be
3 Make sure you show
4 You must arrive on
5 Shake hands
6 Make sure you dress
7 Don't always answer
8 Before the interview, do

a) some research about the company.
b) briefly. Try to give a full response.
c) smartly. Maybe wear a suit.
d) contact. Look at them during the interview.
e) enthusiasm. Smile and ask questions.
f) firmly with your interviewers.
g) prepared. Think about what they will ask you.
h) time. Don't be late!

FUNCTION
TALKING ABOUT YOURSELF

2 A Add the vowels to complete the conversations.

Conversation 1
A: C_ _ld I _sk a q_ _st_ _n?
B: Sure. Go ahead.
A: Will this type of project become common?
B: In my _p_n_ _n, architecture will become more environmentally friendly.

Conversation 2
A: Th_r_ _r_ a c_ _pl_ _f th_ngs I'd l_k_ t_ _sk _b_ _t.
B: OK.
A: How do you see your future in our company?
B: F_ r m_, th_ m_st _mp_rt_nt th_ng is to keep developing and learning the job.

Conversation 3
A: I h_v_ a q_ _ry.
B: Yes? Go ahead.
A: A lot of people criticised you because of the cuts in funding for education. Did you ever think about resigning from the government?
B: One th_ng I'd l_k_ t_ s_y _s th_t compared to other governments, we invested a lot of money in education.

Conversation 4
A: Earlier, you mentioned your latest film. C_n I _sk you _b_ _t th_t?
B: Yes, of course.
A: Was it difficult not being the star?
B: I'd h_v_ t_ s_y 'yes'. In my last four films I always had the biggest part.

B Match pictures A–D with conversations 1–4 in Exercise 2A.

LEARN TO
USE TWO-WORD RESPONSES

3 Circle the correct option to complete the conversations.

1 A: Is it OK if I check my emails?
   B: _____. That's fine.
   a) Go ahead   b) That's right   c) I understand

2 A: Are you interested in free medical insurance?
   B: _____. How do I sign up?
   a) You're correct   b) Yes, definitely   c) No problem

3 A: My dog is ill, so I can't come to work today.
   B: _____. Will you be in tomorrow?
   a) You're correct   b) Please continue   c) I see

4 A: Hi, Nazir. I'm going to be about fifteen minutes late.
   B: _____. There's no hurry.
   a) Yes, definitely   b) That's right   c) No problem

5 A: I can't travel in June – my wife's expecting a baby.
   B: _____. We'll make sure there's no travel until at least August.
   a) I understand   b) Go ahead   c) You're welcome

6 A: Do you live at 106 West Smith Road?
   B: Yes. _____.
   a) That's right   b) No problem   c) You're welcome

7 A: Thank you so much for letting me use your motorbike.
   B: _____. Did you have fun?
   a) Yes, definitely   b) I see   c) You're welcome

8 A: Excuse the interruption. I'm just showing Mr Liu the classrooms. _____.
   B: Oh, OK. So, students, turn to page 33.
   a) I see   b) You're welcome   c) Please continue

9 A: Are you able to work next weekend?
   B: _____. We need to finish the project, don't we?
   a) Go ahead   b) Of course   c) I understand

VOCABULARY
TYPES OF STORY

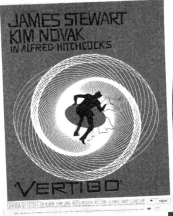

1 A Add vowels to complete the words to describe types of story.

1 Cr_m_ films range from Hitchcock's thr_ll_r *Vertigo* to *Gone Girl*.

2 *The Theory of Everything* is a b_ _p_c of the scientist Stephen Hawking.

3 The most successful ever f_nt_sy film series is *The Lord of the Rings* and *The Hobbit*.

4 I enjoy all film genres, particularly historical or p_r_ _d dr_m_.

5 *Begin Again* is a r_m_nt_c c_m_dy about a woman who goes to New York to work as a musician and meets a man who changes her life.

6 *The Wizard of Oz* is a classic children's _dv_nt_r_ story.

7 *2012*, one of the biggest Hollywood d_s_st_r films ever made, shows the end of the world as we know it. The special effects are truly spectacular.

8 *The Hunger Games* is one of the best ever _ct_ _n films.

9 *The Salt of the Earth* is a d_c_dr_m_ about the life of Brazilian photographer Sebastiao Salgado.

B Which words in Exercise 1A could be used to describe these films?

1 In *What If*, a man falls in love with his best friend but doesn't think he can tell her.

2 *San Andreas* is based on what would happen if there was an earthquake in Los Angeles.

3 *Nowhere Boy* talks about John Lennon while he was at school and art college in 1950s Liverpool.

4 *World War Z* is set some time in the future when a virus has turned much of the world's population into zombies.

5 *Die Hard* stars Bruce Willis as a policeman battling against terrorists.

6 *Murder on the Orient Express*: When his train is stopped by deep snow, detective Hercule Poirot is called on to solve a murder when the body of one of the passengers is discovered.

GRAMMAR
PRESENT PERFECT AND PAST SIMPLE

2 Underline the correct alternatives.

1 A: I've never been/didn't go to Hollywood.
B: Haven't you? I went/'ve been there last year.

2 A: How many films have you acted/did you act in so far?
B: I've acted/acted in seven films up to now.

3 A: He's only twenty-two years old, but he travelled/has travelled all around the world.
B: Which countries did he visit/has he visited?

4 A: She has won/won four Oscars for her performances.
B: That's right. She has won/won an award for Best Actress last month.

5 A: They have lived/lived in California for twenty years.
B: When did they move/have they moved to Texas?

6 A: Have you been/Were you here long?
B: Yes. I arrived/have arrived over an hour ago.

7 A: We've been married/were married for forty years now.
B: Do you remember the day we've met/met?

8 A: Did you enjoy/Have you enjoyed the film?
B: I didn't have/haven't had time to watch it yet.

3 Rewrite the second sentence so that it means the same as the first. Use the correct form of the words in capitals.

1 I met Ella ten years ago. KNOW
I *'ve known* Ella for ten years.

2 She went to Mumbai four weeks ago. BE
She _____ in Mumbai for four weeks.

3 They started the business in 2009. WORK
They _____ together since 2009.

4 We moved into the house six months ago. LIVE
We _____ this house for six months.

5 This is my third visit to London. GO
I _____ three times.

4 A ▶ 2.1 Listen and complete the conversations.

1 A: Have you been here before?
B: Yes, _____ Naples a few times.

2 A: Have you had time to see the museum yet?
B: No, _____ time.

3 A: Did you find your hotel OK?
B: Yes, _____ the hotel without any problems.

4 A: Have you got your guidebook?
B: Oh no. I _____ it in my room.

5 A: Have you had any lunch?
B: Yes, _____ eaten.

6 A: Have you enjoyed your stay?
B: Yes, _____ a wonderful time.

B Listen again and shadow the answers.

VOCABULARY PLUS
PREPOSITIONS

5 Underline the correct preposition to complete the sentences.

1 I'll see you *at/on/in* lunchtime.
2 We often cook outside *at/in/on* the summer.
3 I start work at 8.30a.m. *at/on/in* Monday.
4 I try not to go out alone *at/on/in* night.
5 I just heard it *at/on/in* the radio.
6 *At/On/In* the end, we decided to take a taxi.
7 I'm sorry. I took your coat *at/by/in* mistake.
8 Please be quick. We're *at/by/in* a hurry.
9 Wait there. I'll be with you *at/on/in* a moment.
10 We found the museum completely *at/by/in* chance.
11 I'm afraid Mr Reeves is away *at/on/in* business. Can I help?
12 Nobody wanted to come with me, so I went *at/on/in* my own.

READING

6 A What do you know about James Dean? Are the statements true (T) or false (F)?

1 James Dean became famous for his role in the film *Rebel Without a Cause*.
2 He died in a car accident when he was just twenty-one years old.
3 He was speeding in his car at the time of the accident.
4 When he was younger, he nearly died in a motorcycle accident.
5 His favourite drink was whisky.

B Read the article on the right and check your answers. Correct the false statements.

C Circle the correct option to answer the questions.

1 Why do people come to Hollywood?
   a) Because it's dangerous.
   b) To follow their dreams.
   c) To meet other actors.
2 Why was James Dean nicknamed 'America's Rebel'?
   a) He played a teenager in the film *Rebel Without a Cause*.
   b) He was friends with another actor, Ronald Reagan.
   c) Teenagers respected his rebellious attitude.
3 What did he do before he arrived in Hollywood?
   a) He performed dangerous stunts on television.
   b) He raced motorbikes.
   c) He worked in a restaurant.
4 Why did Dean argue with his father?
   a) His father caught him drinking whisky.
   b) He crashed his father's car.
   c) His father didn't want him to be an actor.

FOREVER YOUNG:
THE HOLLYWOOD HERO WHO DIED YOUNG

'Dream as if you'll live forever; live as if you'll die tomorrow.'

1 The dream is the same for everyone: actors, dancers, singers, film-makers. They go to Hollywood looking for money, success, fame and power. And many come to Hollywood as young people, barely out of their teens. But Hollywood can be a dangerous place, and some of Hollywood's heroes even lose their lives because of it. But although they die young, they are heroes forever, immortalised in film history.

2 One such hero was James Dean. Dean once said 'Dream as if you'll live forever; live as if you'll die tomorrow'. Arriving in Hollywood as a young man, James Dean quickly became a star. In the film *Rebel Without a Cause*, Dean showed teenage angst at its best, and he captured the world with his casual style and rebellious attitude. It was an attitude that he held both on-screen and off, and teenagers everywhere found a hero they could both respect and admire. Soon, he was more popular than even his own screen idol, Marlon Brando, and he was nicknamed 'America's Rebel' by Ronald Reagan.

3 Always the rebel, Dean was afraid of nothing. Before becoming famous, he worked as a stuntman for a TV show. Dean loved his car, a silver Porsche 550 Spyder, and it was in this car that on September 30, 1955, Dean crashed and died from his injuries. He was just twenty-four years old. Even though his career in Hollywood was short, he only made three films, he made a lasting impression on everybody who watched him, and even on future generations. James Dean will be forever young.

4 There are many myths about James Dean, but only some of them are true. James Dean loved speed. When he was younger, he had a motorcycle accident and lost his two front teeth. People assumed that Dean was speeding at the time of his car crash – he had been stopped by police for speeding just two hours earlier. But experts now believe that Dean was travelling at 55 mph, and that the accident was just unlucky. As a young man, Dean was a rebel at home. He was thrown out of his father's house when they argued about Dean wanting an acting career, rather than a career in law. And finally, on-screen James Dean is shown getting into a fight after drinking whisky, but off-screen his favourite drink was coffee.

D Find words or phrases in the text to match definitions 1–5.

1 still very young/in their early twenties (paragraph 1)
   _____
2 made famous for a long time (paragraph 1)
   _____
3 opinions or behaviour which are against authority (paragraph 2) _____
4 an opinion or feeling about someone/something that you have for a long time (paragraph 3)
   _____
5 thought something was true (paragraph 4)
   _____

LISTENING

1 A Read the introduction to a radio programme. Are the statements true (T) or false (F)?

1 A 'flashbulb memory' is a memory of an important event.

2 You do not usually remember small details with a flashbulb memory.

FLASHBULB MEMORIES – WHERE WERE YOU THEN?

Do you remember where you were when an important event occurred? Can you remember who you were with? Then you may have what is called a 'flashbulb memory'. In 1977, two psychologists, Roger Brown and James Kulick, used the term 'flashbulb memories' to talk about people's recollections of the John F. Kennedy assassination. They suggested that, like a camera's flashbulb, when a truly shocking event happens, the brain 'takes a picture' of the moment when you learn about the event. This enables us to remember, sometimes in great detail, events of an emotional significance to us. Tune in to Radio 6 *Real Lives* and listen to some of the stories.

B ▶ 2.2 Listen to the stories. Match pictures A–D with speakers 1–4.

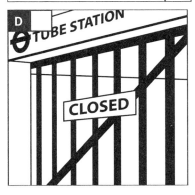

C Listen again and answer the questions.

1 Who was angry about not getting to a meeting on time?
_____

2 Who watched the news on a black and white television?
_____

3 Who got up to make everyone coffee? _____

4 Who were trying to talk on their mobile phones? _____

5 Who thought that maybe what they remembered was just a dream? _____

6 Who wanted peace for everyone? _____

GRAMMAR

NARRATIVE TENSES

2 Circle the correct option to complete the sentences.

1 Simon was feeling exhausted because
   a) the baby wasn't sleeping all night.
   b) the baby hadn't slept all night.

2 We were driving to the hospital to visit Sam when
   a) they called to say she had gone home.
   b) they were calling to say that she was going home.

3 By the time we got to the beach
   a) the rain had stopped.
   b) the rain stopped.

4 Juan was feeling excited because
   a) he wasn't seeing his parents for ten years.
   b) he hadn't seen his parents for ten years.

5 She was singing an old folk song
   a) which I hadn't heard for years.
   b) which I didn't hear for years.

6 Everyone was dancing because
   a) Porto had just won the match.
   b) Porto were just winning the match.

3 Complete the conversations with the correct form of the verbs in brackets.

Conversation 1

A: What ¹_____ (happen) to you on Saturday night? We ²_____ (wait) for ages, but you ³_____ (not come).

B: I'm really sorry. I ⁴_____ (drive) back from Aga's house when my car ⁵_____ (break) down.

A: Why didn't you call?

B: My phone ⁶_____ (run out) of battery.

Conversation 2

A: ⁷_____ you _____ (enjoy) your dinner last night?

B: No. Actually, I ⁸_____ (hate) it.

A: Why? What happened?

B: Well, we ⁹_____ (book) a table, but I ¹⁰_____ (not realise) it was right by the door. People ¹¹_____ (come) in and out all evening and it was freezing. Then, when the waiter ¹²_____ (pour) my wine, he ¹³_____ (spill) it down my dress. And also, we ¹⁴_____ (order) fish, which they ¹⁵_____ (say) was fresh. But when it ¹⁶_____ (arrive) it ¹⁷_____ (taste) terrible!

VOCABULARY

THE NEWS

4 A Complete the headlines with the words in the box.

> crash   demonstration   attacked   strikes
> earthquake   fugitive   floods   hostages

1

Plane _____ in the Mediterranean

2

Thousands killed and more homeless in huge _____ in Haiti

3

Pirates take families as _____

4

HEAVY _____ DESTROY HOUSES AS RIVER WATER RISES

5

_____ arrested at airport

6

Thousands attend anti-war _____

7

PRIME MINISTER _____ WITH EGGS AND ROTTEN FRUIT DURING CONFERENCE

8

Train workers' _____ cause delays

B Circle the correct option to complete the sentences.

1 We need to check our flights. The airport workers are planning _____.
   a) strikes   **b)** demonstrations

2 Protesters _____ the building when they were locked out and caused a lot of damage.
   a) demonstrated   **b)** attacked

3 Police were congratulated when the _____ was finally arrested.
   a) hostage   **b)** fugitive

4 If the rain continues, more _____ are expected.
   a) floods   **b)** earthquakes

5 The driver _____ because he had turned the corner too fast.
   a) crashed   **b)** attacked

WRITING

A NEWS REPORT; LEARN TO USE TIME LINKERS

5 A Put the sentences/paragraphs in the correct order to complete three news reports, A–C. Each report should have three parts:

1 an introductory statement to say what happened
2 background information
3 a concluding statement (or an opinion in quotes).

REPORT A

a _____ The pupils mark their fingerprints [1]*while/as soon as* they enter the church. They will be monitored over three years.

b _____ [2]*During/Until* that time, if they attend 200 masses, they will be excused from taking one exam.

c _____ A Polish priest has installed an electronic reader in his church in Warsaw for school children to leave their fingerprints when they attend mass.

REPORT B

a _____ But Kiyotaka Yamana, a Tokyo resident who started the 'Love Message Yelling Event' after his marriage failed, said that didn't mean they were unromantic. 'The dominant image of Japanese men is of overworked businessmen, but I wanted to tell people around the world that Japanese men are actually very romantic,' Yamana told reporters.

b _____ [3]*While/During* they are on stage, yelling 'I love you' or 'Let me be with you', they are filmed and the event is broadcast on national television. [4]*Until/By the time* recently, Japanese men have usually chosen not to talk very openly about love.

c _____ Love is really in the air in Tokyo at the 'Love Message Yelling Event'. [5]*While/During* the event, dozens of people stand on a stage in Hibiya Park in central Tokyo and shout out love messages to their partners.

REPORT C

a _____ However, [6]*by the time/until* they reached the ruins, the area had been cut off by floods and mudslides and they had to wait [7]*as soon as/until* army helicopters could come and airlift them to safety.

b _____ The travellers had finished the difficult 45-km (28-mile) trek along Peru's Inca trail to see the famous Machu Picchu ruins.

c _____ Over a thousand tourists had to be evacuated from Machu Picchu last week.

B For each report, answer the questions.

1 What happened?
2 Where was it exactly?
3 Why did it happen?

C Underline the correct time linkers to complete the reports.

D Write a short news report (80–120 words) describing a recent news event in your country.

VOCABULARY

SAY/TELL

1 Complete the sentences with the correct form of *say* or *tell*.

1 President Obama _____ a joke and everybody laughed.
2 The manager called to _____ she was sorry about what had happened.
3 I still can't believe that he _____ me such a big lie. I'm furious with him.
4 Someone once _____ me a story about that.
5 Listen. Why don't you just _____ what you mean?
6 As Jodie walked past the table, the young man looked up and _____ 'hello'.

FUNCTION

TELLING A STORY

2 Underline the correct options to complete the story.

STUCK IN THE SNOW

[1]*This happened when/All of a sudden* I was snowboarding with a few friends in Italy. [2]*Before long/Well*, most of the group were really good skiers, [3]*so/in the end* one day we went to the top of this difficult run.
[4]*In the beginning/Anyway*, the field was full of fresh snow and in the middle a tree had fallen down and was covered in snow. It made a perfect jump, so soon everyone was queuing up to perform tricks. [5]*Well/Before long* it was my turn. Well, I went as fast as possible and jumped up ready to do a back flip. But I forgot to bend my knees. [6]*So/The next thing I knew*, I was pointing down, like an arrow. I went head-first into the snow, right up to my waist. My legs were sticking up in the air and I couldn't move. [7]*In the end/Before long*, they had to dig me out. [8]*Anyway/All of a sudden*, we've all laughed about it ever since.

LEARN TO

SHOW INTEREST

3 Complete the conversation with the words in the box.

| what Really no then amazing |
| happened Oh kidding |

A: You'll never guess what happened to Mukul.
B: No. What happened?
A: Well, you know he's working as a taxi driver to help pay for his medical studies.
B: Yes, I know.
A: Anyway, he took a family who were on holiday from Italy in his taxi. And one of his passengers was a seventy-two-year-old grandmother.
B: Yes, so what [1]_____?
A: Well, she left her handbag, with more than $21,000 of the family's travelling money, some very valuable jewellery and some of their passports, in the back of his taxi.
B: Oh [2]_____. You're [3]_____. So, [4]_____ did he do?
A: Well, he looked in the bag to see who it belonged to.
B: Yes, …
A: And he found an address that was fifty miles away. So, he drove all the way there.
B: And what happened [5]_____?
A: Well, there was no one in …
B: [6]_____ dear.
A: So he left a note and his telephone number. And when the family called him, he went back and returned the bag.
B: [7]_____?
A: Yes. As you can imagine, the family were overjoyed and they offered him a reward.
B: How much?
A: I don't know. He didn't take it. He said he couldn't accept it. He was just happy that he'd done the right thing.
B: I don't believe it. That's really [8]_____.

VOCABULARY LANGUAGE

1 Complete the sentences.

1 Sarah uses a lot of _____ and informal words when she speaks – she's a typical teenager.
2 I thought he was British – his English is so good he sounds like a _____.
3 His story was written well but the _____ wasn't good – he made lots of spelling mistakes.
4 I wish I were _____! It must be great to speak two languages from childhood!
5 Living in a _____ country is a great way to learn the language.
6 The teacher was impressed by her _____ and how easily she spoke.

GRAMMAR QUESTION FORMS

2 A Complete the interview questions. Use the same verbs as the answers.

A: Who ¹_____?
B: I work for a small publishing company called Calinet.
A: What type of things ²_____?
B: I do a lot of things – some editing, contacting authors.
A: What problems ³_____?
B: I deal with problems concerning the manuscripts: mistakes, wrong length, wrong style.
A: When ⁴_____ working there?
B: I started working there in 2007.
A: ⁵_____ the job?
B: Yes, I do enjoy it. It's great.
A: So why ⁶_____ for this job?
B: I applied because it's a great company.

B ▶ R1.1 Listen and repeat the questions with the correct intonation.

VOCABULARY RELATIONSHIPS

3 A Match the sentences with the people in the box.

classmate   boss   team-mate   partner
mentor   employee

1 'Please finish this report for me by tomorrow morning.' _____
2 'Ian, can I borrow your pen? I forgot to write my name on my homework.' _____
3 'Come on! Together we can win this game!' _____
4 'Let's look at this together; I can give you some ideas.' _____
5 'I have a meeting in the office with my manager at 6.00.' _____
6 'We'll split the costs 50/50, OK?' _____

B Mark the stress on the words in the box.

GRAMMAR REVIEW OF VERB TENSES

4 Put the verbs in brackets into the correct tense to complete the introduction to a speech.

Hello, everybody! My name is Shane Towers. I ¹_____ (be) a teacher, but at the moment I ²_____ (take) a year off to finish my Master's Degree. I ³_____ (not start) working with children until 2005, but now I ⁴_____ (love) it.

Today I'm going to talk about Theatre of the Oppressed. I first ⁵_____ (see) the name when I ⁶_____ (look) through some articles for my degree. I ⁷_____ (read) an article about drama in education and suddenly the name ⁸_____ (jump) out at me: 'Theatre of the Oppressed'. In my country, the theatre ⁹_____ (not be) usually for or about the oppressed; it's for rich or middle-class people. I ¹⁰_____ (want) to find out more …

VOCABULARY PLUS COLLOCATIONS

5 Complete the sentences with *go*, *take*, *get* or *do*. Use the present simple or the past simple.

1 I ___*did*___ a lot of research before I ___*got*___ my degree.
2 A year ago she _____ up a new hobby: acting. Then she _____ part in her first play.
3 Last night we _____ some work on the proposal and then we _____ for a meal.
4 Can you _____ me a favour? Can you help me to _____ this test?
5 You _____ after your father. I hope you don't _____ grey when you're twenty-five, too!
6 Eventually I _____ off Jane because she always _____ angry for no reason.

VOCABULARY INTERVIEW ADVICE

6 Circle the correct option to answer the questions.

1 How should you dress before an interview?
   a) messily   **b)** brilliantly   **c)** smartly
2 How should you shake hands with someone?
   a) nicely   **b)** firmly   **c)** heavily
3 When should you arrive for an appointment?
   a) on time   **b)** quickly   **c)** late
4 What shouldn't you avoid in an interview?
   a) foot contact   **b)** head contact   **c)** eye contact
5 What should you do before an interview?
   a) some research   **b)** a job   **c)** the washing
6 What should you show in an interview?
   a) your CV   **b)** your photos   **c)** enthusiasm

FUNCTION TALKING ABOUT YOURSELF

7 Read the conversation between Ian and his boss, John. Which lines are correct? Which have an extra word?

I: John, could I to ask a question?	1 ___to___
J: Of course. What would you like to know?	2 ___✓___
I: There are but a couple of things.	3 _____
J: Yes, go ahead.	4 _____
I: I am have a query about the website.	5 _____
J: Yes. You know it isn't finished yet?	6 _____
I: Can I to ask you when it will be finished?	7 _____
J: It's for me, the most important thing is to get it right.	8 _____
I: I understand, but when will it be ready?	9 _____
J: I'd have really to say, websites have been a big problem for this company.	10 _____
I: In the my opinion, they've been the biggest problem. But when will it be ready?	11 _____
J: One thing I'd like for to say is that we are working hard on the website.	12 _____
I: So you don't have a date?	13 _____
J: Er … no. Sorry.	14 _____

LEARN TO USE TWO-WORD RESPONSES

8 Put the words in the boxes into pairs to make two-word responses. Then complete the conversations with the correct responses.

of   problem   welcome   course   no   you're

1 A: Thank you so much.
   B: _____.
2 A: Sorry about that.
   B: _____.
3 A: Can I leave early, please?
   B: _____.

ahead   correct   see   I   go   you're

4 A: I think the answer is 'Paris'.
   B: _____.
5 A: Can I tell you what happened?
   B: _____.
6 A: I couldn't come because I was ill.
   B: _____.

I   right   that's   please   understand   continue

7 A: Is your name John Brown?
   B: _____.
8 A: Sorry I didn't finish it.
   B: _____.
9 A: So, I was telling you about …
   B: _____.

VOCABULARY TYPES OF STORY; THE NEWS

9 Complete the descriptions of films with the words in the box.

fantasy   fugitive   demonstrations   strike   biopic science   earthquake   period   thriller   violent crash   attack   disaster   comedy

1 This _____ describes the life of Cesar Chavez, the leader who organised a workers' _____ so that people could work under fair conditions.
2 This psychological _____ tells the story of a _____ who hides from the police while trying to prove that he is innocent.
3 This is a very funny romantic _____ that tells the story of two people who fall in love when their cars _____ on a small road.
4 This _____ fiction film describes what happens when aliens _____ planet Earth, attempting to destroy everything.
5 This children's _____ begins when a hole opens up in the ground after an _____ and a giant, friendly creature comes out to rescue everybody.
6 This _____ movie tells the story of a _____ storm that destroys the city.
7 This _____ drama tells the story of women fighting for the vote and their _____ on the streets of London in the early 1900s.

GRAMMAR PRESENT PERFECT AND PAST SIMPLE

10 Read the phrases in italics and correct the ones that are wrong.

1 The Berlin Wall *has fallen* in 1989.
2 *Have you been* to any of the Caribbean islands?
3 I started work at 6a.m. but I still *haven't finished*.
4 What time *have you gone* to bed last night?
5 It's so dry here. It *hasn't rained* for weeks.
6 Did you hear about Casey? He*'s broken* his leg!
7 Van Gogh *hasn't sold* many paintings during his lifetime.
8 You're a good guitar player. *Have you played* for long?

11 ▶ R1.2 Listen and tick the sentence you hear.

1 a) I stopped. b) I've stopped.
2 a) We made it. b) We've made it.
3 a) He helped me. b) He's helped me.
4 a) They killed it. b) They've killed it.
5 a) You worked hard. b) You've worked hard.
6 a) I thanked her. b) I've thanked her.

VOCABULARY PLUS PREPOSITIONS

12 Complete the diary entry with the correct prepositions.

> I went ¹_____ a run in the morning while listening to some music ²_____ Eminem. I hate running ³_____ the winter, especially ⁴_____ Monday morning. It's too cold! Unfortunately, Kim is away ⁵_____ business and only gets back late ⁶_____ night, so I had to run ⁷_____ my own. It was hard work running six miles, but I did it ⁸_____ the end. Had breakfast ⁹_____ a hurry and managed to get to work ¹⁰_____ time. Problems with the bus so I went ¹¹_____ train, which was quicker. ¹²_____ chance, I heard ¹³_____ the radio that the new film ¹⁴_____ Roger Graves, an old friend of mine, was coming out ¹⁵_____ June. It's about a man who runs every morning and hates it!

GRAMMAR NARRATIVE TENSES

13 Complete the sentences with the past simple, past perfect or past continuous form (positive or negative) of the verbs in the box. Use each verb once.

> turn on   finish   eat   open   do   leave   stay
> listen   wear   go

1 She went to Hotel Buena Vista, but I _____ in Hotel Primavera!

2 As Bilal closed the door, he realised he _____ the keys in the car.

3 Yannick _____ to music when someone knocked on the door.

4 When I got to work, I saw that I _____ one black shoe and one brown shoe!

5 When we arrived, it was cold because Dad _____ the heating.

6 Bella started the course last year, but she _____ it.

7 Goa was new to us because we _____ there before.

8 It was too hot so I _____ the window.

9 The police want to know what you _____ between 6.30a.m. and 7.00a.m. yesterday.

10 The food tasted horrible, so we _____ it.

VOCABULARY SAY/TELL

14 **A** Complete the phrases with *say* or *tell*.

1 _____ jokes

2 _____ 'hello'

3 _____ a white lie

4 _____ sorry

5 _____ stories

6 _____ what you mean

B Complete the sentences with the correct form of phrases from Exercise 14A.

1 When I was young, my father always _____ before we fell asleep.

2 Most comedians _____ but his face alone makes you laugh!

3 I explained that I didn't mean to break the window! I _____!

4 She isn't very friendly, is she? She never _____ when I see her in the street.

5 He didn't want to make her cry, so instead of telling the truth, he _____.

6 Instead of talking for hours around the issue, why don't you just _____!

FUNCTION TELLING A STORY; SHOWING INTEREST

15 Underline the correct alternatives.

A: ¹*Happened this/This happened* when I was on holiday in Portugal last year. There were three of us renting this old, scary house in the countryside. It was miles from anywhere.

B: So what ²*happened/did happen*?

A: We'd had a really nice evening. My friend is a good cook and she'd made this lovely meal, so we were feeling very content and full. ³*In anyway/Anyway*, that night, just after we'd all gone to bed, we heard this kind of scratching sound at the door. ⁴*To/In* the beginning, we just thought it was the wind and we went to sleep and forgot about it. But then the following night, the same thing: scratch, scratch at the door.

B: ⁵*But no/Oh no*!

A: ⁶*Well/Very well*, we were all in separate rooms but ⁷*after/before* long we were all sitting together in the living room, really scared. ⁸*So/So on* we talked and talked, trying to work out what to do.

B: And what ⁹*did you do/you did*?

A: ¹⁰*Final/Finally* we decided to get a knife or another weapon and go outside together to see what it was. ¹¹*The next thing/The near thing* I knew, I was at the front of three frightened girls, carrying the kitchen knife and about to unlock the front door.

B: ¹²*Dear/Oh dear*!

A: It went really quiet again. And then, all of ¹³*the sudden/a sudden*, there was the scratching sound.

B: So what ¹⁴*happened then/then happened*?

A: I opened the door and a cat jumped back and ran off into the night. All that panic and ¹⁵*for/in* the end it was just a cat!

B: That's really ¹⁶*funny/fun*!

A: Well yes, we all laughed afterwards, but it was very scary at the time!

CHECK

Circle the correct option to complete the sentences.

1 Jose is _____ – he speaks Spanish and English.
   a) monolingual   **b)** bilingual   **c)** multilingual

2 Where _____ last summer?
   a) have you go   **b)** do you go   **c)** did you go

3 What music _____?
   a) do you listen   **b)** you listen to   **c)** do you listen to

4 Who _____ you with this homework?
   a) helped   **b)** did help   **c)** was helped

5 _____ she like pasta?
   a) Is   **b)** Does   **c)** Do

6 I'm _____ a novel.
   a) writing   **b)** be writing   **c)** already written

7 What _____ between 4.00p.m. and 4.30p.m.?
   a) did you do   **b)** were you doing   **c)** you were doing

8 We are _____ of a tennis club.
   a) team-mates   **b)** partners   **c)** members

9 They _____ in a concert.
   a) did   **b)** took place   **c)** took part

10 Can you _____?
   a) make me a favour   **b)** do me a favour   **c)** do me favour

11 You have excellent _____ and learn quickly.
   a) learning strategies   **b)** learning styles   **c)** learning systems

12 I _____ research before I started the project.
   a) did a   **b)** took some   **c)** did some

13 I _____ about this topic.
   a) could question   **b)** ask a question   **c)** have a query

14 Why don't you _____ and tell your story?
   a) go ahead   **b)** be ahead   **c)** go forward

15 _____ me, the most important thing is to be honest.
   a) By   **b)** For   **c)** According

16 I love films about the future, especially _____.
   a) fiction science   **b)** science fiction   **c)** period drama

17 We _____ to Italy yet.
   a) didn't go   **b)** not have been   **c)** haven't been

18 _____ Paul last night?
   a) Were you see   **b)** Did you see   **c)** Have you seen

19 What _____ to your hair?
   a) have you done   **b)** you have done   **c)** you did

20 I didn't want to work _____ my own.
   a) in   **b)** on   **c)** by

21 She fired the gun _____ mistake.
   a) by   **b)** on   **c)** at

22 He realised he _____ Janine before.
   a) met   **b)** was meeting   **c)** had met

23 The alarm went off while we _____.
   a) sleep   **b)** were sleeping   **c)** had slept

24 I was nervous because I _____ a speech before.
   a) wasn't giving   **b)** didn't give   **c)** hadn't given

25 When I _____ her, she didn't know who I was.
   a) had met   **b)** was meeting   **c)** met

26 The kidnappers wanted a million dollars for each _____.
   a) hostage   **b)** fugitive   **c)** flood

27 That boy is always _____ lies.
   a) speaking   **b)** saying   **c)** telling

28 If you did something wrong, you should _____ sorry.
   a) ask   **b)** say   **c)** tell

29 All _____, the rain came down.
   a) in the end   **b)** very sudden   **c)** of a sudden

30 That's impossible – you _____ joking!
   a) must to be   **b)** must be   **c)** must

RESULT   /30

VOCABULARY

ORGANISATION

1 A Match 1–5 with a)–e) to make sentences.

1 Will you be able to **meet**
2 Well I'm ready! Shall we **get**
3 Do you think she's going to **put things**
4 My son always **gets**
5 I'm going to **use my time**

a) **started** and open the meeting?
b) **distracted** when he's doing his homework.
c) **off**? She already has a lot of work to do.
d) **wisely** and check my luggage while I'm waiting for the taxi.
e) **the deadline** on this job or will you be late?

B Match the sentences in Exercise 1A with the responses below. Complete the responses with the words in the box.

| ahead   prioritising   multitasking |
| leave   waste |

1 Don't worry. I'll finish. I don't usually _____ time.
2 Tell him to finish it all _____ of time and then it won't be such a problem.
3 I don't think so. She probably wants to get it done fast and she is pretty good at _____.
4 Good idea as we have limited time. I'd like to start by _____ our most important tasks.
5 Yes, better not to _____ things to the last minute or you'll miss your flight.

LISTENING

2 A ▶ 3.1 Listen to three people talking about planning things. Who thinks he/she:
a) is a procrastinator? _____
b) is a good planner? _____
c) plans too much? _____

B Listen again and circle the correct option.
1 Where is Ruth planning to stay?
   a) in city hotels
   b) in youth hostels
   c) in hostels and cheap hotels
2 What does she plan to do in Lodz?
   a) go out and find artwork
   b) do a city tour
   c) shop in the city centre
3 What has Kieron done to prepare for his trip?
   a) packed his sports bag
   b) booked his bus ticket
   c) written a list of things to pack
4 What does he think he will forget?
   a) his bag
   b) his boots
   c) the tickets
5 What type of party is Amber organising?
   a) a beach party for a diving group
   b) a birthday party at a swimming pool
   c) a birthday party with diving
6 What does Amber enjoy about her job?
   a) arranging large events
   b) scuba diving
   c) meeting new people

C Match the underlined words and phrases in extracts 1–5 with meanings a)–e).
1 I'm afraid I have to organise things in <u>massive</u> detail …
2 … you see them as you <u>wander</u> around the city.
3 I'm going to a sports <u>tournament</u> next week …
4 … we've <u>made it</u> to the final matches.
5 I think planning <u>comes naturally to</u> me.

a) walk around slowly in a relaxed way with no specific purpose
b) be successful in or achieve something
c) do something easily without learning it
d) a competition with different matches leading to a winning team
e) a large amount

Ruth

Kieron

Amber

GRAMMAR

THE FUTURE (PLANS)

3 Underline the correct alternatives to complete the conversation.

A: ¹*Do you go/Are you going* anywhere this weekend?

B: Yes, we ²*'re going/'ll go* up to Edinburgh to see some of the sights.

A: That's nice. Where ³*are you going/might you* to stay?

B: I don't know yet. I ⁴*have/'m going to have* a look online later.

A: I've got some friends in Edinburgh. They ⁵*might/are going to* have some space. I ⁶*'ll give/ 'm going to give* you their number.

B: Thanks. That's great. What about you? ⁷*Do you do/ Are you doing* anything exciting?

A: No, I think I ⁸*'ll spend/'m spending* the weekend watching DVDs.

4 Complete the email. Use the present continuous, *will/might* or *be going to*. There may be more than one possibility.

> Hi Ros
>
> ¹ _____ (you/do) anything at the weekend? Do you want to come out with us? Danny and I ² _____ (go out) on Saturday night. It would be great if you could come. We ³ _____ (try) one of the restaurants in Trastevere – it's really nice round there.
>
> One thing we've planned is we ⁴ _____ (meet) up with a few people from the course for a drink first, in Piazza Santa Maria. Do you know it? We ⁵ _____ (be) outside Café Marzo from about 6.30, if you want to join us. I'm not sure how late we ⁶ _____ (be). If anyone still has enough energy at the end of the evening, a DJ friend of mine ⁷ _____ (play) at the Gioia Music Restaurant, so we ⁸ _____ (go) there and dance a bit afterwards. We'll see how things go. I ⁹ _____ (call) you tomorrow to see what your plans are.
>
> Speak soon,
> Silvia

5 A ▶ 3.2 Listen to the sentences. Which words are stressed? Circle the option you hear.

1 a) They're <u>going</u> to <u>play squash</u>.
   b) <u>They</u>'re going to play <u>squash</u>.

2 a) I'm <u>going</u> to buy a <u>new phone</u>.
   b) I'm going to <u>buy</u> a new <u>phone</u>.

3 a) She's <u>going</u> to <u>spend</u> a week in <u>Greece</u>.
   b) She's going to spend a <u>week</u> in <u>Greece</u>.

4 a) He isn't <u>going</u> to eat <u>anything</u>.
   b) He <u>isn't</u> going to <u>eat</u> anything.

5 a) Are you <u>going</u> to <u>walk</u> to the <u>station</u>?
   b) Are <u>you</u> going to <u>walk</u> to the station?

6 a) <u>He's</u> going to change his <u>job</u>.
   b) He's going to <u>change</u> his <u>job</u>.

B Listen again and repeat. Focus on the pronunciation of *going to* in fast speech.

WRITING

MESSAGES; LEARN TO USE NOTE FORM

6 A Match messages 1–6 with situations a)–f).

1 Gone to lunch. Back soon.

2 Mr Jackson called. No message. Will call again later.

3 Dentist appointment cancelled. Need to rebook.

4 At the cinema. Dinner in the oven. See you later.

5 Messages — Going swimming after school – want to come?

6 Sorry, didn't tidy bedroom – was late for school.

a) a brother leaving a message for his sister
b) a mother leaving a message for her son
c) a secretary leaving a message for his/her boss
d) a colleague leaving a message for other colleagues
e) a son leaving a message for his mother
f) a person leaving a message for self as a reminder

B Which words have been deliberately left out of the messages? Rewrite the messages in full.

1 _____
2 _____
3 _____
4 _____
5 _____
6 _____

C Write notes for these situations.

1 To your boss: Tell him that Mr Ali telephoned and that you have arranged for them to meet at Mr Ali's office tomorrow morning at 9a.m.

2 To your brother: Invite him out to the cinema this evening.

3 To your colleague: Say that you have gone home and will be back in the office tomorrow.

READING

1 Read the text and choose the best heading.
   a) Famous inventions
   b) Man and the planet – what's next?
   c) Science in the future: discoveries

2 Read the text again and answer the questions.

1 Where has space travel taken us?
   _____

2 What kind of energy will we produce?
   _____

3 How will we control the locks and lights in our homes?
   _____

4 What can American scientists already do?
   _____

5 Why will skin and bone grown in a laboratory help people?
   _____

6 Why do some people disagree with space exploration?
   _____

3 Complete the text in Exercise 1 with the following sentences. Write the correct letter in gaps 1–5.

   a) We will no longer need to be physically present to control what happens in our homes.
   b) Some people would prefer technology to be used differently.
   c) Of course at the moment the equipment is large and inconvenient.
   d) These changes will make life easier for people but will offer other advantages, too.
   e) It is hard to believe that only a few years ago computers were not an everyday part of life.

4 Find words in the text to match definitions 1–4.

1 important (paragraph A) _____
2 clever and complex (paragraph D) _____
3 damage to a part of the body such as a hole or cut (paragraph E) _____
4 searching for and finding out about a place (paragraph F) _____

A ¹_____ We now take tablets, mobile communication and other types of new technology for granted. We can speak to friends on the other side of the world as if they were in the same room and see their faces on instant-messaging systems. Space travel is no longer unusual as we explore Mars and beyond. Medical science has produced new ways of curing disease and helped build robotic hands. In the last fifty years, technology has changed the world beyond recognition. Leading scientists believe that technology will continue to change our lives in significant ways. So what can we expect in the next 20 years or so?

B Firstly science will continue to change our homes and the world around us. ²_____ Scientists believe that technology will be key in helping us to protect the environment. New systems will allow cities to become environmentally 'clean'. Resources will be recycled and we will produce energy that does not pollute the environment.

C Houses themselves will become 'smart' with water, electricity and doors being controlled via the internet or our phones. ³_____ We already have the technology to control locks, lights and alarms via phone apps. These will become normal as people use their mobile devices to turn on heating or air conditioning and check security from miles away or even other countries.

D We will continue to use technology to communicate. It is likely that broadband will become so sophisticated we will be able to project images of our friends like holograms when we talk to them. Scientists in the USA have already found a way to project 3D images using sensors, mirrors and video-conferencing pods.

4_____ But they believe that the technology will eventually be good enough and small enough for people to use every day and people will be able to project an image of themselves to wherever they want – a business meeting for example.

E Medicine will continue to improve. Doctors will be able to grow skin, bone tissue and even organs in laboratories to help repair wounds. As scientists understand more about human genes they will be able to cure or prevent illnesses by using this knowledge.

F Of course not everyone is impressed by these developments. ⁵_____ In fact many people believe that science should only be used to prevent hunger, war and disease, and the money spent on computers, space exploration and weapons should be used to improve the world as it is now.

VOCABULARY
FUTURE TIME MARKERS

5 A Complete the predictions with the words in the box.

term	next	~~future~~	in	time	short

1 In the near ___future___ I'm going to travel around Europe. I just need to save a bit more money.
2 The economy is weak now, but it will improve in the long _____.
3 In the _____ term we expect our profits to increase by about 3 percent.
4 I'm planning to get married to my boyfriend _____ a year or two. Then we'll start a family.
5 In ten years' _____ I hope to be a doctor working with children somewhere in Africa.
6 I'm starting a new job _____ month. If all goes well, I'll keep working for the company until I retire.

B Which predictions are about things that will happen soon? Which are about things that will happen more than three years in the future?

GRAMMAR
THE FUTURE (PREDICTIONS)

6 Rewrite the second sentence so that it has the same meaning as the first sentence. Use the words in capitals.

1 There's a possibility that I will study in Spain. MAY
I _may study in Spain_ .
2 Where do you plan to stay? WILL
Where _____ ?
3 Will you speak to Ted tomorrow? GOING
Are _____ ?
4 Janine probably won't pass her exam. UNLIKELY
Janine _____ .
5 The weather forecast predicts a storm. GOING
There's _____ .
6 He has a chance of becoming the champion. COULD
He _____ .
7 Scientists will probably find a cure for cancer one day. LIKELY
Scientists _____ .
8 I don't think we'll be able to attend the meeting. MAY
We _____ .
9 There isn't time for us to go shopping. WON'T
We _____ .
10 There's an opportunity to meet next week. COULD
We _____ .

7 Complete the text with one word in each gap. Contractions are one word.

THE FUTURE OF LANGUAGE LEARNING

In the future we [1]_____ going to see more and more people using technology to learn languages. There will [2]_____ software that gets computers to read texts aloud and translate them. And we [3]_____ only talk on the computer; we will also talk with the computer in any language we choose.

We will also begin to understand the importance of the five senses in language education, and researchers and publishers are likely [4]_____ look at children's toys for inspiration. Music is going [5]_____ play an increasing role in language learning. Short texts and phrases will be set to music and this will help students to remember the words, just as The A, B, C Song helps children learn the alphabet.

Textbooks may [6]_____ unrecognisable when compared to today's books. They will come with microchips that produce smells and sounds. So if we are learning the word bread, when we touch that part of the page it will smell of bread. If we are learning the word cry, when we touch the word it [7]_____ make a crying sound.

At first, these books [8]_____ likely to be expensive, but market economics will drive prices down. So get ready for fun and games while you learn another language – these changes could happen sooner than you think!

VOCABULARY PLUS
IDIOMS

8 Underline the correct alternatives.

'I always put my [1]foot/hand in it when I speak to people. Socialising is really not my cup of [2]tea/coffee. I love my friends, they're really close to my [3]head/heart, but I'm quite shy with strangers.'

'I joined the [4]mouse/rat race last year when I became a project manager. I have to keep my [5]ear/eye on three or four projects at the same time. We're always [6]working/running against the clock and quite often we [7]work/run out of time. My friend said I was constantly multitasking and he [8]kicked/hit the nail on the head – there is always something to do.'

'I thought an online course would be a [9]piece/bit of cake, but I soon found myself in [10]cold/hot water. It was really difficult. I work hard but, let's [11]face/eye it, sometimes that isn't enough. So I asked for some advice from another guy. He was an A student and he gave me a [12]foot/hand with one of the assignments and I passed the course.'

FUNCTION

DEALING WITH MISUNDERSTANDINGS

1 Put the underlined words in the correct order to complete the sentences.

1 I tried to call you but <u>wrong it number was the</u>.

_____

2 Sorry! <u>realise didn't I</u> it was your birthday!

_____

3 He was late because <u>date he wrong the got</u>.

_____

4 I didn't know it was you – <u>recognise didn't voice your I</u>.

_____

5 We emailed but in fact <u>different was a it person</u> with the same name.

_____

2 ▶ 3.3 Cover Exercise 3. Listen and match pictures A–C with conversations 1–3.

LEARN TO

REFORMULATE

3 Listen again and complete the conversations.

Conversation 1

A: Hello? I'm trying to find my lost luggage.

B: Ah, OK.

A: My bags went missing in Montevideo in Uruguay, after a flight from Curitiba, Brazil.

B: ¹_____ you say that ²_____? Montevideo?

A: I flew from Curitiba to Montevideo and my bags went missing.

B: Have you reported it already?

A: Yes, the name is Anders Kleeburg.

B: Hang on. Could you ³_____ the last name? Anders … ?

A: Kleeburg. K-l-e-e-b-u-r-g.

Conversation 2

A: OK, so cricket. So this is the bowler, OK? He runs up and bowls at the batsman.

B: ⁴_____ exactly do you ⁵_____? What's a bowler?

A: A bowler is the person with the ball in his hand, OK? And he tries to get the batsman out. Get him off the field.

B: Do you mean to ⁶_____ he tries to kill the batsman with the ball?

A: No!

Conversation 3

A: Did you read this?! About popcorn. In 1948, two American scientists found some popcorn in a cave in New Mexico and dated it. It was over five thousand years old.

B: I didn't ⁷_____ any of that. Are you talking about popcorn?

A: Yeah, it's an ancient food. Popcorn is thousands of years old.

B: I don't ⁸_____ what you're ⁹_____. You mean the popcorn we ate in the cinema yesterday is thousands of years old!

A: No! Popcorn in general. People have eaten it for thousands of years.

4 Put B's words in the correct order to complete the conversations.

Conversation 1

A: I'm afraid you have to wear a tie in this nightclub.

B: we / can't / saying / in / you're / so / come

_____
_____

Conversation 2

A: The show starts at nine o'clock.

B: you / at / it / starts / didn't / ten / o'clock / say / ?

_____
_____

Conversation 3

A: The pass mark for this exam is seventy percent.

B: what / failed / mean / so / we / you / is

_____
_____

Conversation 4

A: This type of car is twice as expensive as the other one.

B: me / do / costs / to / that / tell / you / it / mean / €50,000 / ?

_____
_____

Conversation 5

A: No other team can catch us.

B: the / words, / we / in / are / other / champions

_____
_____

VOCABULARY
PERSONAL QUALITIES

1 A Complete the words about personal qualities.

1 He won the election because he is a
g_____ c_____. People enjoy
listening to him talk.

2 Susan's h_____-w_____ nature
helped her through university, when she had to
study a lot.

3 Tim started at the bottom of the company, but
he was a_____. He knew that one day he
would be the manager of the whole organisation.

4 Lucy's a very g_____ l_____. She
listens to people and then decides what's best
for everyone to do.

5 He hates to lose a race. He's very c_____.

6 I find it difficult to make decisions. I'm a bit
i_____.

7 You need to be more creative and think
o_____ t_____ b_____.

8 They are a group of very m_____
students. They are keen to work hard.

9 Being a racing driver, Anton has to be a
r_____ t_____. He isn't afraid of
danger.

B Find words or phrases in Exercise 1A which have
the underline{opposite} meaning to 1–8.

1 makes decisions easily ___indecisive___

2 not interested in competing with others
_____

3 lazy _____

4 thinks the same as everyone else _____

5 doesn't communicate well _____

6 not good at organising a team of people
_____

7 doesn't like dangerous situations _____

8 not interested in becoming successful
_____

GRAMMAR
MUST/HAVE TO/SHOULD (OBLIGATION)

2 Match sentences 1–10 with sentences a)–j). Then
underline the correct alternative.

1 We *don't have to/shouldn't* wear a uniform at
work.

2 You *shouldn't/have to* stay up all night studying.

3 I think you *should/mustn't* talk to your boss.

4 You *don't have to/mustn't* drink and drive.

5 I think he *mustn't/should* start his own company.

6 Nurses *have to/should* work long hours.

7 You *don't have to/mustn't* cheat during the exam.

8 I *must/don't have to* leave at 4 o'clock.

9 You *should/don't have to* apologise for his
behaviour.

10 We *should/must* remember to book the tickets
today.

a) He's very ambitious.

b) You need to find out why he shouted at you.

c) It wasn't your fault.

d) You'll be thrown out of the college.

e) We can wear whatever we want.

f) It'll be too late if we wait until tomorrow.

g) It's against the law.

h) Otherwise I'll miss my train.

i) You'll be too tired tomorrow.

j) It's no good if you want a nine-to-five job.

3 Correct one mistake in each sentence.

1 You must to tell him as soon as possible.

2 I've finished this exercise. What I should do now?

3 The clients don't has to come to the office. We
can meet them at the restaurant.

4 I shouldn't to tell you this, but the boss is leaving
on Monday.

5 Do we have wear a uniform?

6 Everybody must leaving the building by 6p.m.

7 She have to be at work by 7.30a.m.

8 I think you should to check what time the film
starts.

9 You don't must use a mobile phone in the
classroom.

10 We have wait until the IT man comes to fix the
system.

LISTENING

4 **A** Look at the pictures. What qualities do you think are important for these jobs?

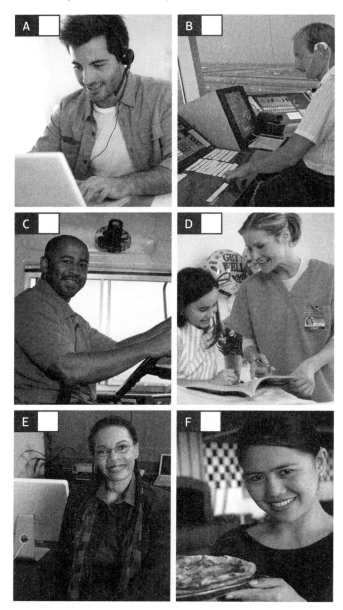

A

B

C

D

E

F

B ▶ 4.1 Listen to six people talking about their jobs. Match pictures A–F above with speakers 1–6.

C Listen again. Who says these things? Write the number of the speaker next to each statement.

1 You have to be organised and have a good memory, too.

2 And you need to pay attention to detail.

3 You shouldn't get stressed too easily.

4 You have to care about the people you're looking after.

5 You always have to be on time.

6 And you have to be able to work well under pressure.

7 You must be very accurate and observant. *1*

8 You have to be able to stay calm.

VOCABULARY PLUS

CONFUSING WORDS

5 **A** Complete the conversations with the words in the box.

job work remember remind forget leave
hear listen fun funny

1 A: Oh no, _____ to that. It's raining and I don't have an umbrella.
  B: Why not? Did you _____ it at home?
  A: Yes, I did.
  B: Here. Use mine.

2 A: Can you _____ me to post that letter on the way home?
  B: Sure. Just _____ to bring it with you.

3 A: Did you have a good night last night?
  B: Yes, it was really _____. We danced until two in the morning, but today I feel terrible.

4 A: I got the _____, by the way.
  B: Congratulations! That's brilliant news.
  A: Yes, I'm so excited. Finally, I'm going to earn a proper salary.
  B: That's great. Well done.

5 A: I've got to go to _____ now. I'll see you later.
  B: Yes, don't _____ we're meeting Chaz at 7.30.
  A: Don't worry. I'll be there.

6 A: Did you _____ the joke about the scarecrow?
  B: No.
  A: He won an award for being outstanding in his field.
  B: That's not even _____.

OUTSTANDING

B Complete the sentences with words from Exercise 5A.

1 Can you _____ me to call my brother later? It's his birthday.

2 Did you _____ about that couple who won millions of pounds on the Euro lottery?

3 I don't get paid enough. I need to get a new _____.

4 We're having a meeting tomorrow morning. Don't _____!

5 I really enjoy my _____. I find it interesting, and the people I work with are good _____.

6 He's so _____. He always makes me laugh.

DREAM JOB turns into NIGHTMARE

1 It was advertised as the best job in the world. And it certainly looked good. You would be paid ($189,000 for six months) to surf, sail and swim. The job came with a beachside mansion, with its own swimming pool, and fantastic views of the ocean. All you had to do was look after tiny Hamilton Island, situated off the coast of Queensland. Duties included feeding the fish and writing a blog of your experiences to help encourage tourism in the area. There were more than 34,000 applicants for the job from all over the world, so Ben Southall was delighted when he beat them all and won the contract.

2 But, as it turned out, it wasn't quite the dream job that some people might have expected. Firstly, it was incredibly busy. Ben found himself working seven days a week and up to nineteen hours a day. He had a busy schedule of events to attend, with promotional events, press conferences, training courses and administrative duties. 'It has been very busy, busier than most people would have imagined, and certainly busier than I had imagined,' Mr Southall told reporters when he finished his contract.

3 In fact, during his six months, Ben visited ninety 'exotic locations', made forty-seven video diaries and gave more than 250 media interviews – including a chat with popular US TV host Oprah Winfrey. He also posted more than 75,000 words in sixty separate blogs, uploaded more than 2,000 photos and 'tweeted' more than 730 times.

4 That didn't leave much time for surfing, sailing or simply relaxing and enjoying the sea views. And when he did get the chance to try out his water sports, things didn't always go well. On one trip, Ben was stung by a deadly jellyfish. Irukandji jellyfish are transparent and very small, so they are very difficult to see in the water.

5 In his blog, Ben describes how he was enjoying jet skiing with some friends, when as he climbed off the jet ski, he felt a sting on his arm. Within thirty minutes, Ben was feeling the venom. He was hot and sweaty, with a headache, pains in his chest and high blood pressure. Ben had to be rushed to a doctor who diagnosed the symptoms and gave him some medication. Luckily, Ben was fine, but it was an unwelcome end to his stay in paradise, and not how he expected to spend his last few days on Hamilton Island. Ben was lucky to survive.

6 However, he still insists that he enjoyed himself immensely. In fact, Tourism Queensland is offering him a new contract, and he will also write a book about his experiences.

READING

1 A Ben Southall got a 'dream job': looking after Hamilton Island, off the coast of Queensland, Australia. The article describes how the job turned into a nightmare. Which of these problems do you think it will mention?

loneliness	free time	feeling bored
problems with animals	illness
money	other

B Read the article to see if you were right. Then answer the questions.

1 What three things help to make the job 'the best job in the world'?
_____

2 Why was the job not as 'ideal' as it seemed at first?
_____

3 What happened to Ben towards the end of his contract?
_____

4 What is he going to do now?
_____

2 Tick the things which Ben did as part of his job.

1 gave speeches
2 made video diaries
3 managed a big team of people
4 gave interviews
5 attended press conferences
6 learned a new language
7 met politicians
8 wrote a novel
9 wrote a blog about his experiences
10 learned to surf and sail

3 Find words or phrases in the text to match definitions 1–8.

1 a large house by the sea (paragraph 1) _____

2 a plan that includes a lot of things to be done in a short time (paragraph 2) _____

3 meetings at which someone answers questions asked by people from newspapers, television, etc. (paragraph 2) _____

4 activities involved in managing the work of a company or organisation (paragraph 2) _____

5 posted a comment using the website Twitter (paragraph 3)
_____

6 have an opportunity (paragraph 4) _____

7 taken very quickly (paragraph 5) _____

8 very, very much (paragraph 6) _____

VOCABULARY
EXTREME ADJECTIVES

4 Complete the sentences with the correct word.

1 a) I thought the show was *brilliant/boiling*.
   b) Is the heating on? It's *brilliant/boiling* in here.
2 a) Have you heard the news? Isn't it *terrible/furious*?
   b) All the trains were delayed. I was *terrible/furious*.
3 a) I'd invite you round, but my apartment is *delicious/tiny*.
   b) Have you tried these salads? They're *delicious/tiny*.
4 a) I can't do it – it's *exhausted/impossible*!
   b) I'm going home. I'm *exhausted/impossible*.
5 a) It's a(n) *fascinating/enormous* story of naval history.
   b) $50,000! That's a(n) *fascinating/enormous* amount of money!

GRAMMAR
USED TO, WOULD

5 Complete the paragraphs. Use one word for each gap.

'I used ¹_____ work for a big company. I ²_____ to work long hours and I ³_____ dream of living in a more exotic location, sitting on a beach with my laptop. Now I run my own website business. I don't earn as much money as I ⁴_____ to earn, but I'm much happier.'

'I ⁵_____ to work as a computer programmer. Most of the time, I ⁶_____ enjoy it. But I didn't ⁷_____ to like being in an office all day. So, I decided to get a job working outdoors. Now, I train people in forestry skills, so I'm outside most of the time. And my lifestyle is much healthier than it ⁸_____ to be.'

6 A Rewrite the sentences with *used to*.

1 Did you spend your holidays by the sea?
_____

2 We didn't have a dog when I was a child.
_____

3 I loved reading in the evening, but now I'm too tired.
_____

4 I remember how I sat in my grandfather's studio and watched him paint.
_____

5 Children always played around on the streets in the old days, but there's nobody here now.
_____

6 They lived in a big house, but they had to move.
_____

B Tick the sentences in Exercise 6A where you could replace *used to* with *would*.

7 A Look at the underlined words. Are they pronounced with a /s/ or /z/ sound?

1 I <u>used</u> to be very sporty.
2 Can I <u>use</u> your phone?
3 He never <u>used</u> to worry about it.
4 I <u>used</u> to live in the USA when I was 18.
5 This stuff is <u>used</u> to kill insects.
6 I don't <u>use</u> the car much any more.
7 We <u>used</u> to love going there on holiday.
8 I didn't <u>use</u> to live in Europe.

B ▶ 4.2 Listen and check. Then listen and repeat. Focus on the pronunciation of /juːstə/.

WRITING
A COVERING LETTER; LEARN TO ORGANISE YOUR IDEAS

8 A Put the covering letter in the correct order.

☐ Thank you for your consideration. If you require any further information, please do not hesitate to contact me. I can be reached at vinniej22@dmail.com or 07788 922 123. I look forward to hearing from you ¹<u>soon</u>.

1 Dear Ms Nelson,

☐ I believe that my communication skills, customer service abilities and positive work ethic would make me an asset to the shop.

☐ I am currently studying English at Exeter University and I am looking for summer work to help me finance my studies. ²<u>I think I would be good at this job</u>. Firstly, I am both hard-working and organised, and I have excellent communication skills. Secondly, I have ³<u>shown that I am good at</u> customer service. In my previous job, on the reception desk at Queen's Hospital, I had ⁴<u>practical</u> experience of providing quality customer service and working with all types of people.

☐ Yours sincerely,

☐ I am writing to you ⁵<u>about</u> the summer position at SunnySam's Electronics, advertised on www.summerjobs⁴students.com. ⁶<u>I want to apply</u> for the post. I attach my CV, application form and all the information required in the advertisement.

☐ Vinnie Jessop

B Replace the underlined sections 1–6 in the letter with the phrases in the box. Write the correct number.

hands-on ☐ at your earliest convenience ☐
regarding ☐ proven ability at ☐
I would like to submit an application ☐
I believe I meet all the requirements of the post ☐

C Write a covering letter (120–180 words) for a summer job working as a restaurant/shop manager.

VOCABULARY
BUSINESS

1 **A** Circle the correct options to complete the text.

Hi Lucy,

I'm just writing to tell you about my new job. Remember when I had to go for [1]_____ last month? Well, I got the job. I'm so pleased about it, because I heard a lot of people were [2]_____ for it, probably because it has quite a high [3]_____.

The people in the office are really good fun and it is such a relief not to be out of [4]_____ any more. My new boss is in [5]_____ of the whole marketing department and she [6]_____ it really well. She has lots of really interesting business [7]_____ and encourages us to try and do the same. The only problem now is that I still arrive late for work all the time. I hope I don't get [8]_____.

Let me know how you're getting on at work.

Speak soon.

Becca

1	**a)** an interview	**b)** a job	**c)** a work
2	**a)** working	**b)** attempting	**c)** competing
3	**a)** salary	**b)** money	**c)** holiday
4	**a)** work	**b)** salary	**c)** employ
5	**a)** control	**b)** charge	**c)** lead
6	**a)** works	**b)** is	**c)** runs
7	**a)** thoughts	**b)** ideas	**c)** posts
8	**a)** interview	**b)** boss	**c)** fired

B Use the phrases in Exercise 1A to complete the sentences.

1 I'm lucky to work there – lots of people _____ to get jobs there.

2 Would you prefer to earn a high _____ or do something interesting?

3 My boss _____ the business very successfully and it's growing every day.

4 He behaved so badly I'm not surprised that he was _____.

5 I hate it when I have to do an _____ – I get nervous.

6 My cousin has been out of _____ for ages. She doesn't have any money.

FUNCTION
REACHING AGREEMENT

2 Complete the conversation with the phrases in the box.

not sure that I agree   suggest we think about
see what you mean   see things
that's a good idea   How about if we   That's fine

A: The way I [1]_____, the first thing we need to do is update the website.

B: Yes, [2]_____. But we haven't decided what information to put there.

A: I know. I [3]_____ what should be on the site and then decide who's going to work on it.

B: [4]_____ by me.

C: I'm [5]_____, actually. I think we need to look at the finances first. We don't know how much money we can spend on the website yet.

B: I [6]_____, but I'm not sure what to do. [7]_____ decide what we would like first and then look at how much it will cost?

C: Fine. That sounds good to me.

LEARN TO
MANAGE A DISCUSSION

3 Complete the sentences with the words in the box.

on (x2)   all   recap   to   up

1 Let's focus _____ the main problems and talk about the rest if we have time.

2 OK, but first of _____, we need to look at the notes from the last meeting.

3 Moving _____ to the next point. What are we going to do about salaries?

4 So, let's _____ on the main ideas we've discussed and then we'll stop for lunch.

5 I think we need to come back _____ the decision to relocate.

6 Let's sum _____ what we've talked about.

GRAMMAR THE FUTURE (PLANS)

1 Circle the correct option to complete the sentences.

1 I'm working hard so that I _____ the deadline.
  a) meet
  b) do
  c) find

2 Let's _____ started and not waste time.
  a) make
  b) try
  c) get

3 I usually prioritise _____ at the start of the day.
  a) tasks
  b) time
  c) job

4 I hope you aren't going to _____ off doing that!
  a) put
  b) place
  c) stop

5 Concentrate please! Don't _____ distracted.
  a) been
  b) get
  c) have

6 Who _____ invite?
  a) will you
  b) will you going to
  c) you might

7 Peter _____ fifty on Saturday!
  a) is being
  b) is going to be
  c) might be

8 _____ a Thai curry. I'm expecting about twenty people.
  a) I'm going to cook
  b) I will to cook
  c) I'm cooking

VOCABULARY ORGANISATION; FUTURE TIME MARKERS

2 A Complete the sentences with the words in the box.

> ~~meet~~ gets multitask last get distracted of prioritise time use

1 I always try to _____*meet*_____ my deadlines and finish my work without delays.

2 My friend usually leaves things till the _____ minute.

3 Can you get your homework done ahead _____ time if possible?

4 She is a great manager. She always _____ meetings started on time.

5 Don't waste _____ with small jobs – focus on the most important ones.

6 I like to _____ things done as well as possible.

7 He is really easily _____ from the main task.

8 If you can _____ your time wisely, you will get more done.

9 If you have small children, you have to learn to _____ and do several things at once.

10 I don't know which tasks to _____ in this project.

2 B Underline the correct alternatives.

1 We'd like to buy our own house in a *term/year* or two.

2 In the long *term/year*, I think she made the right decision.

3 I'd like to start my own business at some point in the future, but that will be a *short/long* time from now.

4 In the *short/long* term, over the next few weeks, we want to see business improve.

5 In ten *next/years'* time, I hope to be a surgeon.

6 *Next/Years'* month, we will celebrate twenty years of marriage.

GRAMMAR THE FUTURE (PREDICTIONS)

3 Underline the correct alternative to complete the text.

THE FUTURE OF DRIVING

So, with improvements in technology and people becoming more and more environmentally aware, what is the future of motorised transport? We asked some experts for their opinions.

Matthew G – car salesman, USA

'Honestly? I think things [1]*aren't likely to/are going to* change a lot. People [2]*may/might not* like it, but governments [3]*may/aren't going to* introduce more laws and taxes to 'punish' people who use their own cars instead of public transport. This [4]*is going to/isn't going to* force people to leave their cars at home and some people might even sell their cars. It's already happening and I think in the future this trend [5]*won't to/is likely to* continue.'

Ian M – bus driver, UK

'I think the future [6]*will/is likely* be very different. Vehicles [7]*couldn't/won't* need people to drive them. I think they [8]*are going/may* have robot drivers, so people like me will have to find different jobs. I think we [9]*are going to/may not* see more and more cities begin to use buses like this. There [10]*might/couldn't* be fewer jobs for lorry drivers, too, as companies won't have to pay people to transport their products.'

VOCABULARY PLUS IDIOMS

4 Write the second sentence so that it means the same as the first. Use idioms which include the words in capitals.

1 It's so easy. CAKE
It's _____.

2 He was in trouble. WATER
He was _____.

3 I said something really inappropriate. FOOT
I put _____.

4 It's an issue which is very important to me. HEART
It's an issue which is _____.

5 He left his job in the city to go and become a coffee farmer. RAT
He decided to leave _____
and become a coffee farmer.

6 Could you help me sort out these papers? HAND
Could you _____
sorting out these papers?

7 I am trying to lose weight. FACE
_____,
I'm a bit too heavy at the moment.

8 I don't really like R&B music. TEA
R&B music isn't _____.

9 I like to follow what's happening in politics. EYE
I like to _____
what's happening in politics.

10 I'm afraid we have no more time. RUN
I'm afraid we've _____.

FUNCTION DEALING WITH MISUNDERSTANDINGS; REFORMULATING

5 Complete the conversations with the words in the box.

saying	mean	catch	get	other	repeat	what
say	exactly	lost				

1 **A:** The picture dates back to the sixteenth century when it was ...
B: I didn't _____ any of that.

2 **A:** So, you take the third turning on the right, go straight on for 200 metres, turn left, take the first right again and it's straight in front of you.
B: I'm sorry. You've _____ me.

3 **A:** If you don't have a pink stripe on your ticket, then I'm afraid staff are not allowed to let you in.
B: Apologies, but I'm afraid I don't _____ what you're saying.

4 **A:** We had a very minor incident involving your new car.
B: What _____ do you mean?

5 **A:** We are sorry to report that all trains have been cancelled.
B: Do you _____ to say we can't travel today?

6 **A:** I've come to collect a parcel for Mr Wainwright.
B: Can you _____ that again?

7 **A:** There's one stop-over, for twenty-four hours, in Bahrain.
B: Could you _____ the last thing you said?

8 **A:** This desk is now closed.
B: So, you're _____ that we need to move to another desk?

9 **A:** I'm afraid you need to vacate the premises.
B: So _____ you mean is we need to go?

10 **A:** We anticipate inconveniences along the route.
B: In _____ words, we're going to be late.

VOCABULARY REVIEW

6 Complete the words in the sentences.

1 He always wants to win. He's very co_____.

2 Part of being a good le_____ is being able to listen to people.

3 It's one of the most am_____ films I've ever seen. It's very moving.

4 I have to go to bed as soon as possible. I'm absolutely ex_____.

5 To be a successful entrepreneur, you need to be a ri_____ ta_____.

6 It's minus ten degrees outside. It's fr_____!

7 It's a fa_____ story, really interesting. It's about a man who …

8 I love my job, but I should be earning a much bigger sa_____.

9 He was always telling the bo_____ what to do and in the end, he got fi_____.

10 I'm very nervous, because I've got to go for this job in_____ tomorrow.

11 I can't believe how angry he was. He was absolutely fu_____.

12 I'm sure she'll do well in her new job. She's very ha_____-wo_____.

7 A Put the words in the box into the correct place in the table according to the stress pattern.

amazing salary tasty competitive successful leader interview furious delicious boiling difficult freezing exhausted impossible

oOo	Ooo
amazing	*salary*
Oo	**oOoo**

B ▶ R2.1 Listen and check.

GRAMMAR MUST/HAVE TO/SHOULD (OBLIGATION)

8 Complete the sentences with the correct form of *must, have to* or *should*. Use the information in brackets to help you.

1 Milo _____ write three ten-thousand-word essays for his course. (It's necessary)

2 We _____ tidy up the house. Jenna will be home soon. (It's a good idea)

3 You _____ park here. You'll get a fine. (obligation not to do this)

4 You _____ pay for children. They can come in for free. (It isn't necessary)

5 The sign says you _____ keep your dog on a lead. (It's necessary)

6 You _____ smoke anywhere in the building. It isn't allowed. (obligation not to do this)

7 You _____ wear a helmet when you ride your motorbike. It's the law. (It's necessary)

8 Do children _____ go to school on Saturdays? (Is it necessary?)

9 You _____ wear jeans to a job interview. (It isn't a good idea)

10 You _____ pay for the coffee. It's free. (It isn't necessary)

VOCABULARY PLUS CONFUSING WORDS

9 Complete the sentences with the words in the box.

listen	funny	remember	remind
hear	fun	forgotten	left

1 I'm sorry. I can't _____ your name. Is it Sarah or Sue?

2 I've _____ how this machine works. Please can you show me again.

3 It's in my bag, which I've _____ in the car.

4 You never _____ to what I'm saying.

5 Sorry, the music's too loud. I can't _____ you.

6 Can you _____ me to stop at the bank on the way home?

7 I always laugh at his stories. He's so _____.

8 Why don't you come with us to the restaurant? It should be _____!

GRAMMAR USED TO, WOULD

10 A Complete the text with *used to* or *would* and the verbs in brackets. Where both *used to* and *would* are possible, use *would*.

FIVE YEARS AGO

Greg and Emily Bishop [1]_____ (live) on a small island in the Caribbean. They had a wonderful life. Greg [2]_____ (work) as a teacher in a local school, and Emily [3]_____ (study) for an online course at a university. They [4]_____ (have) a house on the beach and after school, the children [5]_____ (play) on the beach with their friends. At the weekends, they [6]_____ (enjoy) surfing, sitting on the beach and eating delicious tropical fruit, like mangoes and pineapples. But when Greg's father became ill, the family decided to move back to the UK.

B Read about Greg and Emily's life now. Then complete sentences 1–6 with *used to* or *would*.

NOW

Greg runs his own taxi company and Emily has a job working in a sports centre. The children don't enjoy school as much and say they have to wear too many clothes all the time to keep warm. At the weekends, they all stay inside and watch football on television and eat fish and chips.

1 Greg _____ (not have) his own business.

2 Emily _____ (not work) in a sports centre.

3 The children _____ (enjoy) school more in the Caribbean.

4 The children _____ (not wear) so many clothes to keep warm.

5 The family _____ (not stay) inside at weekends.

6 They _____ (eat) tropical fruit, not fish and chips.

FUNCTION REACHING AGREEMENT

11 A Complete the phrases in the conversation with the words in the box.

don't	sure	suggest	need	about	what	things	that
me	point	agree	should				

A: OK. As you all know, we had record sales last year, and we'd like to organise a celebration for all the staff. Any ideas for what we could do?

B: Well, I feel [1]_____ we should have a party here in the office.

A: That's OK by [2]_____.

C: I'm not sure that I [3]_____, actually. I think we [4]_____ think about going somewhere else. The way I see [5]_____, we spend every day in the office. Why [6]_____ we do something different to celebrate?

D: That's a good [7]_____. How [8]_____ if we go on a trip somewhere?

B: Yes. Or we could do a course together. There's a place where you can go and make chocolates, or bake bread or something like that.

D: I'm not [9]_____ that's a good idea. I [10]_____ we focus on things we all enjoy doing, like sport. [11]_____ about spending a day playing golf?

C: Golf! I don't think so.

A: OK. I think we [12]_____ to focus on whether we have a party of some kind or go on a trip somewhere.

B Which phrases are used to give opinions? Which are responses to a suggestion or idea?

CHECK

Circle the correct option to complete the sentences.

1 Hi, Jake. What _____ this evening?
   a) you doing   **b)** are you doing   **c)** will you doing

2 I'm not sure. I think I _____ stay at home and study.
   a) will to   **b)** might   **c)** going to

3 We _____ Italy for our holidays. We love it there.
   a) are going to   **b)** will go   **c)** might going

4 I always want to _____ things done as quickly as possible. I hate time wasting.
   a) have   **b)** make   **c)** get

5 I hate doing my banking so I'm very easily _____.
   a) prioritised   **b)** distracted   **c)** changed

6 He's changing his job in a month or _____.
   a) term   **b)** year   **c)** two

7 I think it will be better for everyone in the long _____.
   a) year   **b)** term   **c)** time

8 Look at the sunshine! You _____ have a great time at the beach.
   a) 're going to   **b)** 're likely to   **c)** may

9 We _____ never see him again.
   a) aren't likely to   **b)** may   **c)** won't

10 Yes, we're working against the _____ to finish in time.
   a) pressure   **b)** life   **c)** clock

11 I was really late home even though my dad told me not to be. I'm in really _____ water.
   a) dark   **b)** hot   **c)** dirty

12 We don't know much about him. He's a dark _____.
   a) horse   **b)** dog   **c)** fish

13 She's very lazy. The boss told me to keep an _____ on her and check she's working.
   a) sign   **b)** note   **c)** eye

14 I'm sorry. I didn't _____ you were busy.
   a) recognise   **b)** remind   **c)** realise

15 I'm afraid I didn't _____ that. Can you say it again?
   a) catch   **b)** take   **c)** do

16 André is very _____. He wants to sell his designs all over the world.
   a) lazy   **b)** ambitious   **c)** indecisive

17 Françoise is a good _____. People really listen to what she has to say.
   a) risk taker   **b)** listener   **c)** communicator

18 The doctor said I _____ take these pills.
   a) has to   **b)** have to   **c)** haven't to

19 Help yourself to anything you want. You _____ ask.
   a) don't have to   **b)** have to   **c)** must

20 It's a wonderful _____. I enjoy it a lot.
   a) work   **b)** study   **c)** job

21 I can't believe how big your kitchen is. It's _____.
   a) tiny   **b)** big   **c)** enormous

22 The interview was _____. I'll never get the job.
   a) brilliant   **b)** awful   **c)** exhausting

23 When I told my boss, he was _____.
   a) furious   **b)** terrible   **c)** impossible

24 As children, we _____ play at the bottom of the garden.
   a) used   **b)** use to   **c)** would

25 My mother _____ live in the mountains.
   a) used to   **b)** use to   **c)** would

26 If we work as a _____, we'll get the job done faster.
   a) boss   **b)** businessman   **c)** team

27 More than a hundred people had to _____ for a single job.
   a) compete   **b)** decide   **c)** get fired

28 The way I see _____, we need to start again.
   a) point   **b)** things   **c)** idea

29 That's OK _____ me.
   a) on   **b)** at   **c)** by

30 I think we need to sum _____ what we've learned.
   a) up   **b)** on   **c)** at

RESULT   /30

5 SOLUTIONS

LISTENING

1 A ▶ **5.1** Listen to Mia, Tom and Owen answering the following questions. Write M (Mia), T (Tom) or O (Owen) next to the question they answer.

1 How has your country changed in the last thirty years? _____

2 Is the world getting better or worse? _____

3 How has your life changed in the last thirty years? _____

B Circle the correct option to complete the sentences.

1 Mia thinks that thirty years ago _____.
   a) life was simpler
   b) the pace of life was faster
   c) people were happier

2 Mia thinks that email puts pressure on people because _____.
   a) people's computers crash
   b) emails sometimes don't arrive
   c) we are expected to give an instant response

3 Tom says that Beijing has grown because people _____.
   a) don't have as much money as before
   b) came from around the world to get rich
   c) came from all over China to make money

4 Tom says that life in the countryside _____.
   a) has changed enormously because of new technology
   b) will never change because they do not have access to technology
   c) has not changed that much, but people have more technology

5 Owen says that living conditions around the world _____.
   a) are improving, even though many people are still living in terrible poverty
   b) are terrible and are going in the wrong direction
   c) are not improving, and more and more people are living in poverty

6 Owen thinks that there are _____.
   a) fewer wars than before, but weapons are getting more dangerous
   b) more wars than before, and weapons are getting more dangerous
   c) the same number of wars as before, and weapons are getting safer

C Listen again and check.

GRAMMAR

COMPARATIVES AND SUPERLATIVES

2 Complete the conversation with the correct form of the adjectives in brackets.

A: I love my new digital camera. It was
¹_____ (expensive) my last one, but the pictures are much ²_____ (good) quality and it's ³_____ (easy) to use.

B: But it's much ⁴_____ (big). Isn't it ⁵_____ (heavy) to carry around with you?

A: Actually, it was one of ⁶_____ (light) models in the shop. Although you can get ⁷_____ (small) and ⁸_____ (cheap) cameras, they're not as good as this one.

3 Underline the correct alternatives.

WHAT'S YOUR FAVOURITE GADGET IN THE KITCHEN?

My favourite gadget in the kitchen is the dishwasher. It's ¹*much/a lot more* faster than me at washing up. The problem is that I'm getting ²*a slightly/a little bit* lazier.   **Yuri**

The toaster. Morning is ³*by far/slightly* the best time of the day for me. I enjoy a relaxing breakfast. And toast is ⁴*a lot/more* tastier than bread. I love it.   **Katia**

I don't cook very much, because I'm too busy. I have a microwave, which I find makes it ⁵*more/a bit* easier. Now, I eat ⁶*slightly/a little far* better than I did before.   **Nguyen**

VOCABULARY

TECHNOLOGY

4 A Underline the correct alternative.

1 He's six months old. He's been to the doctor to get his *genetic engineering/vaccinations*.

2 We are running out of coal, so the government is looking at new ways of making *electricity/computer networks*.

3 The government is planning to build new *nuclear power/genetic engineering* stations, but many people are worried that they are too dangerous.

4 The company has just invested thousands of dollars in its new *computer network/antibiotics* to improve communication between employees.

5 It sounds like you've got a chest infection. I think you need some *solar power/antibiotics*.

6 NASA has decided to restart its *communications satellites/space travel* programme and try to send people to Mars.

7 They rode their *commercial aeroplanes/motorbikes* right up through to the United States and Canada. The trip took several weeks.

B Match words in italics from Exercise 4A with definitions 1–8.

1 The science of changing the genes of a living thing _____

2 The energy created when you split or join two atoms _____

3 Drugs used to kill bacteria and cure infections _____

4 Power carried by wires and used to make lights and machines work _____

5 Exploration of the area beyond Earth where the stars and planets are _____

6 Machines that are sent into space and travel around the Earth, sending radio and television signals _____

7 Energy from the sun _____

8 An injection given to someone to protect them from a disease _____

5 **A** Put the words in the correct column according to the pronunciation of the underlined letter *a*.

space ~~antibiotics~~ nuclear travel machine communications satellites vacuum commercial aeroplanes solar vaccinations

/eɪ/ make	/æ/ apple	/ə/ polar
space	antibiotics	

B ▶ 5.2 Listen and check. Then listen and repeat.

WRITING

AN ADVANTAGES/DISADVANTAGES ESSAY; LEARN TO USE DISCOURSE MARKERS

6 **A** Look at the task below and the notes a student has made. Tick the advantages and cross the disadvantages.

> Discuss the advantages and disadvantages of studying English online, as opposed to in a classroom.

1 flexibility – can study where and when you want, don't have to travel to a school

2 lack of interaction with your teacher or students

3 more choice – can choose to skip parts of the course, focus on other parts

4 IT problems – need to be confident with how the technology works, have good connections to the internet, etc.

5 discipline and time management – have to stay motivated

6 materials are technologically advanced – use a variety of multimedia materials

B Look at the two plans, A and B, for the essay. Which is better? Why?

Plan A

Many people now study English online. There are lots of good materials on the internet for doing this. As the technology improves, more and more people will try online learning.

But there are some problems, too. Online learning is boring because you are on your own. It's difficult to be motivated.

My opinion – I have tried online materials and they are very good. But going to a class is a better way to improve your English.

Plan B

Introduction:
Improvement in technology means many people are now choosing to study English online, not in classrooms.

Advantages:
- increased flexibility
- increased choice of materials

Disadvantages:
- lack of interaction with teacher and students
- difficulty with motivation and discipline
- IT problems

Conclusion:
- Online courses offer students more choice and flexibility, but are more impersonal.
- Language is about communication, so face-to-face interaction with people in a classroom is a better way to learn.
- Online courses might be a good way to supplement your learning.

C Look at the essay one student wrote. They forgot to use any discourse markers to link their ideas. Rewrite the essay, including discourse markers from the box where you see an asterisk (*).

> One of the main advantages is that
> Another disadvantage is   The problem is that
> However, (x2)   In my opinion,   And another thing,

With the improvement in technology, many people are now choosing to study English online, rather than in the classroom. It's easy to see that there are many advantages to online courses. * There are also disadvantages.

* When you study online, you have increased flexibility to study when you want to and where you want to. You have an increased choice of the materials you want to study, because you can choose them yourself.

* When you study online, there is a lack of interaction with your teacher and students. * You might find it difficult to stay motivated and be disciplined with your studies. * You might experience computer problems, which make your study difficult.

* Online courses offer students more choice and flexibility. * They are more impersonal. As language is about communication, face-to-face interaction with people in a classroom is a better way to learn.

VOCABULARY
INFORMATION

1 Cross out the alternative which is <u>not</u> possible in each sentence.

1 The class had a really good *debate/discussion/reply* about the environment.

2 He's sure he's right so if you disagree with him, he will *argue/quarrel/inquire* about it.

3 You should try to *respond to/argue/reply to* emails as quickly as possible.

4 I *questioned/looked into/inquired about* renting a car, but it was too expensive.

5 My brother and I always *argued/quarrelled/replied* about everything when we were young.

6 I've always *wondered about/questioned/quarrelled* this man's motivation.

7 The *look into/research/investigation* was a waste of time; we found no solutions.

8 His newspaper column *debates/inquires/discusses* the issues of the day.

2 Add the missing letters to complete the text.

WHO GOES FIRST?

Everyone involved in medical ¹re*search*_____ is eventually faced with a difficult ²qu_____: who will be my guinea pig? Who will be the first person to try this new medicine before we know if it works?

If we ³l_____ i_____ the history of drug testing, we find that many researchers not only ⁴de_____ this issue, but that a few have a surprising ⁵re_____; they use themselves as guinea pigs.

When scientist Jonas Salk was ⁶in_____ a new polio vaccine in the 1950s, he tried the drug on himself, his wife and children. It worked. Someone later ⁷in_____ about who held the patent (the right to sell the medicine). Salk's ⁸re_____ showed his character: he ⁹wo_____ why anyone wanted to make money from something that the world needed.

GRAMMAR
QUESTION TAGS

3 Underline the correct alternative.

1 You're from France, *aren't you/weren't you*?

2 She broke a world record, *hasn't she/didn't she*?

3 They haven't seen us, *have they/haven't they*?

4 Don won't tell anybody, *does he/will he*?

5 That house looks nice, *isn't it/doesn't it*?

6 We didn't see that film, *did we/saw we*?

7 It hasn't rained for months, *has it/have it*?

8 You will come tomorrow, *won't you/will you*?

9 The shop doesn't open at 6a.m., *will it/does it*?

10 You stopped smoking last year, *didn't you/you didn't*?

4 Read the situations and write questions. Use the correct question tags.

1 You think your friend is in love.
You *really like Mary, don't you*? (really like / Mary)

2 You leave the cinema laughing together.
That film _____? (be / funny)

3 Your friend's younger brother is going to borrow your car.
He _____? (not crash / the car)

4 You leave the football stadium after a boring match.
It _____? (not be / very good / game)

5 You say goodbye to your friend at the airport.
You will _____? (write / to me)

6 You want to check that your friend got home safely last night.
You _____? (not miss / the last bus)

7 A tourist thinks you speak French.
You _____? (speak / French)

8 You have lost your watch.
You _____? (not see / my watch)

5 A Read the conversations. Which responses are genuine questions (where Speaker B really doesn't know the answer)?

1 A: Have you met Yinka's parents?
B: Only once. They're doctors, aren't they?

2 A: There isn't a cloud in the sky.
B: I know. It's a beautiful day, isn't it?

3 A: Are you looking for the scissors?
B: You haven't seen them, have you?

4 A: Have you read Jhumpa Lahiri's new book?
B: Yeah, she's a great writer, isn't she?

5 A: I've got my final exam tomorrow.
B: You'll pass, won't you?

6 A: I think this is the wrong address.
B: Yes, we've made a mistake, haven't we?

B ▶ 5.3 Listen and check. Then listen again and repeat the responses. Use the same intonation in the question tags.

READING

6 **A** Read the introduction to the article. Which questions can you answer? Which can only be answered by experts?

I NEVER KNEW THAT!

What is worse for you: boredom or stress? Why is sea air good for you? If you throw water into the air during the Russian winter, will it come back down as ice? What three foods should you take to a desert island?

People love trivia*. In 2005, a book called *Does Anything Eat Wasps?* was a surprise hit. It was a collection of questions and answers from readers of a magazine called *New Scientist*. We at *Lynx Mag* decided to come up with our own questions and then we asked a panel of experts for answers.

*trivia: unimportant facts

B Read the rest of the text to find the answers.

1: You are going to stay on a desert island for several months and you can only choose three foods to take with you. Which do you choose, and why?
Broccoli, walnuts and orange juice. Broccoli has a chemical which helps detoxify your liver. It's also a superfood. Walnuts have protein and plenty of healthy fats. Orange juice is a source of clean water, and the orange contains Vitamin C.   *Dr Leah Morecombe*

2: What's worse for you: boredom or stress?
Boredom. Stress can have benefits. Weightlifting is a type of stress. So are other sports and pressures at work. All of these are good for you in small doses. Boredom means you have no purpose in life, and no dose of boredom is good for you.   *Dr Samran Naipaul*

3: Why is sea air good for you?
It isn't particularly. It got a reputation for being good for you in Victorian times because there was so much unhealthy smog in big cities.   *Dr Robina Whitman*

4: Why do flies like rotting food?
Flies like rotting food because soft environments provide perfect conditions for breeding. When a fly's eggs hatch, the larvae live in and eat the rotting food until they grow into adult flies.   *Dr Kelvin Marsh*

5: If you throw water into the air during the Russian winter, will it come back down as ice?
It depends where you are in Russia and what the temperature is at the time. But, potentially, yes. At a temperature of -30°C, small amounts of water will turn into ice almost immediately.   *Immanuel Kanevsky*

C Complete the questions for the answers.

1 Q: _____ helps detoxify your liver?
   A: Broccoli.
2 Q: What does the writer say _____ ?
   A: It can be good for you, while boredom can't.
3 Q: Who thought sea air was _____ ?
   A: The Victorians.
4 Q: What creatures live in and _____ ?
   A: Fly larvae.
5 Q: At -30°C, when will a small _____ ?
   A: Almost immediately.

D Find words in the text in Exercise 6B that match meanings 1–5.

1 remove dangerous chemicals or poison from something (paragraph 1) ____detoxify____
2 measured amounts of something that you experience at one time (paragraph 2) _____
3 unhealthy air that is full of smoke and pollution (paragraph 3) _____
4 going bad; becoming soft and useless (paragraph 4) _____
5 when an egg breaks and a baby bird, fish or insect comes out (paragraph 4) _____

VOCABULARY *PLUS*

WORD BUILDING: ADJECTIVES

7 Complete the text with the correct form of the words in brackets.

THE PNEUMATIC TYRE: HOW DID IT START?

John Dunlop, a Scottish vet, was [1]_____ (response) for one of the world's great inventions.

Dunlop's young son kept falling off his tricycle because the bumpy streets were [2]_____ (hope) for cycling. Dunlop thought of a [3]_____ (create) solution: filling the rubber tyres with air. This, he realised, would be an [4]_____ (ease) way to make the tricycle more stable. He was right: it turned out to be a very [5]_____ (effect) solution. Lots of cyclists copied the idea and the air tyre became very [6]_____ (success). French car makers realised it was a [7]_____ (value) idea and produced air-filled car tyres. The tyres also became very [8]_____ (profit); Dunlop Tyres is still a huge company today.

VOCABULARY

PROBLEMS AND SOLUTIONS

1 Complete the sentences with the words in the box.

> memory switching crashed sort work print
> down order recharging fixing

1 I'm on the motorway and my car's broken _____.
2 My phone isn't working. The batteries need_____.
3 We can't use the machines here because they're out of _____.
4 Can you call the maintenance department and tell them that the photocopier needs _____?
5 If it still doesn't work, try _____ it off and on again.
6 I don't believe it! My laptop's just _____ again!
7 Have you got another pen? This one doesn't _____ any more.
8 Don't worry about that now. I'll _____ it out later.
9 OK. First, you'd better save the documents onto a _____ stick.
10 I've got a copy on my computer. Do you want me to _____ you a copy?

FUNCTION

POLITE REQUESTS

2 A ▶ 5.4 Listen to eight conversations. What does the person want each time? Match pictures A–H with conversations 1–8.

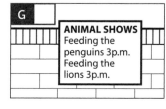

B ▶ 5.4 Listen again. Complete the conversations with one word in each gap.

1 A: Excuse me, _____ you tell me the way to the swimming pool, please?
 B: Yes, of _____ I can. You keep going this way, until you get to the traffic lights. Then, …
2 A: Hello. Do you _____ what time the bank opens?
 B: I'm not _____. I'll just ask someone.
3 A: Do you want us to bring anything?
 B: That would be great. Could _____ bring some salad, and maybe something for dessert?
 A: Yes, _____ course. Anything else?
 B: No, that'll be fine.
4 A: Could you _____ me with my bags?
 B: I'm _____, I can't. I've got my hands full.
5 A: Would you mind _____ the door for me?
 B: Of course _____. There you are.
 A: Thank you. That's very kind.
6 A: Could you _____ me what time the show starts?
 B: _____ me have a look. The afternoon show starts at 3p.m.
 A: Thanks very much.
7 A: Would you _____ coming to get me from the station?
 B: OK. _____. Wait outside and I'll be there in ten minutes.
8 A: Do you know _____ there's a post office near here?
 B: Yes, _____ is – there's one just along this road.

LEARN TO

RESPOND TO REQUESTS

3 Put the words in the correct order to make responses.

1 A: Would you mind saying that again?
 B: of / not / no, / course
 _____

2 A: Do you know how to get there?
 B: sure. / not / I'm / look. / me / have / a / let
 _____

3 A: Could you phone Tilly for me?
 B: course / yes, / of
 _____

4 A: Could you finish doing this for me?
 B: can't / I / afraid / I'm
 _____

5 A: Could you take these folders for me?
 B: I / yes, / can
 _____

VOCABULARY

-ING/-ED ADJECTIVES

1 A Underline the correct alternative.

1 In three days we cycled 250 km. It was really *exhausted/exhausting*.
2 Everyone is very *worried/worrying* about losing their jobs.
3 The instructions were so *confused/confusing* that no one understood them.
4 I was *annoyed/annoying* because the class was cancelled again.
5 The car was travelling at a *frightened/frightening* speed.
6 I felt *embarrassed/embarrassing* about how untidy the house was.
7 He was totally *confused/confusing* by the tax form.
8 I'm going to have a nice, *relaxed/relaxing* bath.
9 I'm not really *satisfied/satisfying* with the way he cut my hair.
10 We were so *frightened/frightening* by the film we didn't sleep very well.

B Find adjectives in Exercise 1A to match definitions 1–8.

1 feeling fear _____
2 angry or irritated _____
3 very tiring _____
4 content, pleased _____
5 unclear or difficult to understand _____
6 feeling uncomfortable and shy _____
7 unhappy and nervous _____
8 calming, helping you to rest _____

READING

2 A You are going to read an article about why people get angry, and what happens. Before you read, number the events in the box according to categories 1–3 below.

1 Reasons   2 Consequences
3 Solutions

You start to shout. *2*
You're irritated with someone. *1*
You throw things around.
You do physical exercise.
You're frustrated about something.
You feel tense.
You try meditation.
People criticise you.
You distance yourself from the situation.

B Read the article and check.

Stressed out?
TAKE CONTROL

We all know how it feels to get angry. Sometimes anger is mild, when you're just irritated with someone. But at other times anger can be more extreme, with explosive rages. You start to shout and throw things around. You lose control. Your blood pressure increases, your heart races and you can't think about anything else. But what exactly *is* anger?

Anger is a normal response to a situation where you feel you are being attacked, treated unfairly, let down by others, hurt or rejected. Anger can help you to defend yourself, deal with the problem and let others know how you feel. But anger can also cause problems. If you always lose control, people might start to avoid you. Friends and colleagues may be afraid of your temper and leave you alone. Getting angry might make you feel better; giving you energy and making you feel like you're in control. But it might also leave you feeling hurt and misunderstood. Also, getting angry doesn't usually solve the problem.

So, what can you do about your anger?

1 Work out what makes you angry – You need to understand what situations make you angry. Is it when people make comments about your work or criticise you? Is it that you get angry when you're frustrated and can't do the things you want? Do you get angry when you're tired? Understanding what makes you angry can help you to deal with the problem.

2 Understand the signals – Learn to identify the signs that you're getting angry. Do you start to shout and feel tense? Do you pace about the room? You need to recognise your own signs before you can change your behaviour.

3 Take control of your mind and body – Try taking a step back and distancing yourself from the situation, both physically and emotionally. Check your breathing and take some deep breaths to slow you down and calm your heartbeat. Ask yourself, 'Am I overreacting?', 'Am I listening to what people are saying?' Can you find a way to be assertive, rather than aggressive? Try to speak calmly, rather than shout. Try the 'Is it worth it?' test. Ask yourself, 'Will it really matter in one month, one year?' Do some physical exercise, like going for a run or a swim. Or try some meditation or listen to music. Do whatever helps to calm you down.

3 Complete the statements with information from the article.

1 When you get angry, your blood pressure _____ and your heart speeds up.
2 Being angry about something can help others to _____ how you feel.
3 Getting angry is not usually a good way to _____ problems.
4 It's a good idea to understand what _____ make you angry.
5 If you recognise the signs that you are getting angry, then you can start to _____ your behaviour.
6 When you are angry, you should try to _____ yourself from the situation.
7 Deep _____ will help to calm your heartbeat.
8 Try to speak _____ rather than shout.

GRAMMAR

REAL CONDITIONALS

4 A Complete the sentences with the correct form of the verb in brackets.

1 When Marianne _____ (find) a job, she _____ (leave) home.
2 Thomas _____ (get) a promotion if he _____ (work) harder.
3 If people _____ (exercise) regularly, they tend to _____ (live) longer.
4 If we _____ (leave) early enough, we _____ (miss) the traffic.
5 We _____ (start) the meeting as soon as everybody _____ (be) here.
6 If the music _____ (be) loud, people always _____ (dance).
7 When the weather _____ (be) good, we usually _____ (eat) outside.
8 If you _____ (use) sun cream, you _____ (not get) burned when we go sailing.

B For each sentence in Exercise 4A, decide if the situation is general (what normally happens – zero conditional), or specific (a possible situation in the future – first conditional).

1 *specific – first conditional* _____
2 _____
3 _____
4 _____
5 _____
6 _____
7 _____
8 _____

5 Tick two correct sentences. Correct the wrong sentences.

           will
1 If I find the book, I ⋏ send it to you.
2 If you will go to England, you will improve your English.
3 I'll tell him you called when I will see him.
4 If you give the plant too much water, it will die.
5 If they arrive early, will you to ask them to wait?
6 If you will come to the party tonight, will you bring a friend?
7 When I go to Krakow, I usually will see my aunt.
8 I always call my sister when there's a problem.
9 She will get angry if you will say that!
10 I go to the doctor tomorrow if I feel worse.

VOCABULARY *PLUS*

MULTI-WORD VERBS

6 A Circle the correct option to complete the sentences.

1 Don't forget to _____ when you've finished.
  a) click on   **b)** take off   **c)** log off
2 She's my best friend. We _____ really well.
  a) get off   **b)** get over   **c)** get on
3 I used to love Indie music, but then I _____ it.
  a) went off   **b)** got on   **c)** logged off
4 I _____ lots of different outfits, but I didn't like any of them.
  a) tried off   **b)** dressed up   **c)** tried on
5 You have to _____ your shoes when you go inside.
  a) log off   **b)** take off   **c)** dress down
6 He's nearly forty. It's about time he _____.
  a) settled down   **b)** went off   **c)** got on
7 Can you _____? I can't read what it says at the bottom of the screen.
  a) scroll on   **b)** scroll over   **c)** scroll down
8 I don't like going into bars on my own. I'm worried someone will try to _____.
  a) get on with me   **b)** chat me up
  c) settle down with me

B Complete the multi-word verbs with a suitable particle.

1 I'd love to settle _____ and have children.
2 Unfortunately, I don't get _____ with his mother very well.
3 A very good-looking young man started to chat me _____ in the nightclub.
4 I think he went _____ me when he met my family!
5 Why don't you try _____ this shirt? I think it will really suit you.
6 Scroll _____ to the top of the page to find our contact details.
7 Do you mind if I take _____ my jacket? It's boiling in here.
8 Sorry, I didn't realise you needed the computer. I've just logged _____.

VOCABULARY

VERB–NOUN COLLOCATIONS

1 Complete the sentences with a verb from Box A and a noun from Box B.

A

watch jump hold get raise do cut

B

sale queue money hair experiments programme seat

1 The scientists in our lab _____ a lot of _____ to find cures for common illnesses.

2 Did you _____ that _____ about UFOs on TV last night?

3 If you don't get to the show early, you won't _____ a _____.

4 The shop manager decided to _____ a _____ of last year's products.

5 Excuse me, you can't _____ the _____. Lots of people are waiting.

6 I asked my sister to _____ my _____ because I couldn't afford the hairdresser.

7 We're trying to _____ _____ for Save the Animals. Our target is €10,000.

GRAMMAR

HYPOTHETICAL CONDITIONAL: PRESENT/ FUTURE

2 Rewrite the sentences using the second conditional.

1 Joe goes to bed at 2a.m. He feels tired all the time.
If Joe *didn't go to bed at 2a.m., he wouldn't feel tired all the time.*

2 She doesn't play for the team – she isn't fast enough.
If she _____

3 We can't drive to your house because we don't have a car.
We _____

4 I have a supportive family. My life is so easy.
My life _____

5 I'd love to buy that house, but I don't have the money.
If I _____

6 I'm so lazy. I don't write to my friends.
I _____ lazy.

7 You don't water your plants regularly. They look dry!
If you _____

8 Tom and Dave never help in the house. Their mother doesn't ask them.
They _____

9 I work on Saturdays. I can't come to the barbecue.
If I _____

3 Put the verbs in brackets into the correct form. Use *would* or the past simple.

Henrik

Lulu

Olly

Brigitte

If you could choose any three things, what three things ¹ _would make_ (make) your life better? We asked this question to the public.

Henrik, 25, from Sweden, said, 'If I really ² _____ (have) a chance to change three things, they ³ _____ (be) the environment, poverty and peace. My priority? I ⁴ _____ (introduce) new laws to save the planet.'

Lulu, 30, from Edinburgh, had different ideas. She said, 'My life couldn't be better, but if I ⁵ _____ (have to) change something, I ⁶ _____ (change) the colour of my curtains – they're a horrible grey!'

Olly, 16, from London, said, 'OK, if I ⁷ _____ (be) able to change three things, first thing: I ⁸ _____ (be) Prime Minister. Second thing: I ⁹ _____ (make) rich people pay more tax. Third thing: I ¹⁰ _____ (not let) people smoke cigarettes because they give you cancer.'

Brigitte, 19, from Germany, immediately said, 'More money! If I ¹¹ _____ (be) richer, I ¹² _____ (not have) to work in this stupid shop! I could spend my days painting, which is my real dream!'

4 A ▶ 6.1 Listen and write the sentences you hear. Write contractions as one word.

1 _____ (9 words)
2 _____? (8 words)
3 _____ (10 words)
4 _____ (10 words)
5 _____? (9 words)
6 _____ (8 words)

B Listen and repeat the sentences. Pay attention to the rhythm and the contractions.

LISTENING

5 A ▶ 6.2 **Listen to the introduction to a radio programme. What is the topic?**

B Look at the picture. Which people do you think are 'potential victims'? Why?

C ▶ 6.3 **Listen to the rest of the programme and check.**

D Listen again and complete the notes.

> POTENTIAL VICTIM?
>
> 1 Woman with dog: _No_, because dogs are _unpredictable_.
>
> 2 Woman on mobile phone: _____, because she isn't _____
>
> 3 Tourists looking at map: _____, because they are concentrating on the map, not _____.
>
> 4 Man leaving cashpoint: _____, because he didn't put the money _____
>
> 5 Woman in mini-skirt: _____, because of her positive _____
>
> 6 Big man in coat: _____, because he's looking at his feet and he doesn't know _____.
>
> 7 Couple leaving taxi: _____, because rule number one of the street is: if you have anything valuable, _____

WRITING

AN EMAIL OF ADVICE; LEARN TO QUALIFY WHAT YOU SAY

6 A Read the problem and choose the best summary.

   a) Kathy doesn't want her friend to apply for a job because it is Kathy's 'dream job'.

   b) Kathy's friend is angry because they both want to apply for the same job.

   c) Kathy wants the same job as her friend, but she is worried their friendship will end if she gets it.

> Last week my colleague and best friend Mariela saw a job advertised in the paper. She told me it's her 'dream job' and she intends to apply for it. Unfortunately, it's also my dream job and I really want to apply. I have more experience than Mariela and would probably have a better chance of getting the job. But if I got it, it would ruin our friendship. Should I apply? And if I do, should I tell Mariela?
>
> *Kathy*

B Put the paragraphs in the correct order to make an email of advice.

Paragraph 1: _____

Paragraph 2: _____

Paragraph 3: _____

Paragraph 4: _____

> ### Dear Kathy
>
> **A** How would you feel if you didn't apply, she did, she got the job and you spent the rest of your career in the same job bored and unhappy? Or how would you feel if, because of her getting this new job (which you *didn't* apply for), she lost daily contact with you and your friendship broke up anyway? Wouldn't that be much worse than both of you applying and supporting each other?
>
> **B** I know that close friendships can be ruined because one person becomes more successful than another. It happens all the time, and not only in Hollywood or on Wall Street. But this is no reason for you not to chase your dreams. Finally, here are a few questions for you.
>
> **C** If she knows this, then that's the end of your problem. All you have to do is be honest with her and tell her that you want to apply. Then see what she says. If she is really angry, <u>perhaps</u> she isn't such a good friend. If I were you, I would also support *her* application as much as you can. Maybe offer to read through her CV and her application letter. If she gets an interview, give her a 'good luck' card and buy her a new pair of earrings to wear on the day. It's possible that neither of you will get the job, but tell her you'll be happy if either of you gets it.
>
> **D** OK, so you work together and are best friends, too. This means that Mariela probably knows how you feel about your job and, in all likelihood, also knows your plans for your career. In all probability, she realises that this job is your dream job, too.

C Read paragraphs C and D again and underline six words/phrases for qualifying what you say. The first has been done for you.

D Read the problem. Write an email of advice (180–200 words).

> In one month, an old friend of mine is getting married. He told me the date nearly a year ago. Unfortunately, I forgot this date and I have now booked a holiday with my new girlfriend on exactly the same day. I can't change the dates of the holiday because my girlfriend can only have this one week off. Her boss says she can't change the date. I really don't know what to do. Help!
>
> *Stefan*

VOCABULARY

LIFE EVENTS

1 A Complete the sentences with the words in the box.

split   lost   pass   won   bought   accident   degree
offered   place   promoted   engaged   failed

1 Did you _____ all your exams?
2 Sam had an _____ at work and had to go to hospital.
3 My boyfriend gets on so well with my boss that he even _____ him a job!
4 Are you going to apply for a _____ at university?
5 Liz and Tony have been _____ for years, but they still aren't married.
6 Tom _____ his job at the factory.
7 I _____ my driving test six times!
8 My parents _____ up when I was three.
9 She _____ an international dance competition.
10 Helen got _____ to manager.
11 He's got a _____ in physics.
12 Last year they _____ a house on the beach in Brazil.

B Match 1–6 with a)–f) to make phrases.

1 pass   **a)** an accident
2 get   **b)** your job
3 win   **c)** with a partner
4 have   **d)** a competition
5 lose   **e)** promoted
6 split up   **f)** exams

FUNCTION

GIVING NEWS

2 A ▶ 6.4 Listen and match conversations 1–8 with situations A–H.

B Cross out one unnecessary word in each sentence. Then listen again and check.

1 Bad news, as I'm afraid.
2 I'm sorry for to have to tell you, but we lost the match.
3 I've got some good unfortunately news for you.
4 I'm afraid of I've got some bad news.
5 There's something who I've got to tell you.
6 You'll never guess what is happened.
7 It's unfortunately, we were burgled last night.
8 I've got something for to tell you.

LEARN TO

RESPOND TO NEWS

3 Complete the words in the responses.

1 A: I've just passed my motorbike test!
  B: C_____! That's f_____ news.
2 A: Maciej's had an accident.
  B: That's t_____! I'm really s_____ to hear that.
3 A: I've just won the race!
  B: W_____ d_____. That's g_____ n_____.
4 A: He was attacked outside his house.
  B: That's a_____! Do they know who did it?
5 A: Amazing! I've just found €100 in an old coat pocket.
  B: H_____ you? You l_____ thing!
6 A: Unfortunately, he didn't get a place at university.
  B: That's a sh_____. I'm sorry to hear that.
7 A: I just bumped into Samantha on my way here.
  B: You're j_____! What's she doing here?

GRAMMAR COMPARATIVES AND SUPERLATIVES

1 Rewrite the second sentence so that it means the same as the first. Use the prompts in brackets.

1 (slightly / warm)
The sea isn't as cold as it was yesterday.
The sea _____ than yesterday.

2 (far / expensive)
These black trainers are much cheaper than those white ones.
Those white trainers _____ these black ones.

3 (delicious)
I have never eaten a meal as good as that one.
That was _____ I've ever eaten.

4 (lot / easy)
I expected the exam to be more difficult.
The exam _____ I had expected.

5 (simple)
All the other solutions to the problem are more complicated.
It's _____ solution to the problem.

6 (much / happy)
I felt terrible yesterday, but today I feel much better.
I'm _____ today than I was yesterday.

7 (bit / short)
My brother is slightly taller than me.
I'm _____ my brother.

8 (bad)
Grandad thinks the world was a better place when he was young.
Grandad thinks the world is _____ it was when he was young.

VOCABULARY TECHNOLOGY

2 Add vowels to complete the words.

1 I don't believe it. The __l__ctr__c__ty has gone off again.

2 He had to have a v__cc__n__t__ __n against measles.

3 I think sp__c__ tr__v__l is a complete waste of money.

4 I worry about g__n__t__c __ng__n__ __r__ng. I don't think we know enough about it.

5 We've put two huge s__l__r p__n__ls on the roof.

6 They're putting in a new c__mp__t__r n__tw__rk to improve communication.

7 N__cl__ __r p__w__r is dangerous because people make mistakes.

8 The region has much more tourism now that c__mm__rc__ __l __ __r__pl__n__s can fly here.

VOCABULARY INFORMATION

3 Underline the correct alternative.

1 I'd like to *discuss/inquire* this with my boss.

2 He didn't *quarrel/respond* to my email.

3 We need to *look/question* into the problem.

4 I'm *wondering/responding* if he'll take the job if we offer it to him.

5 I need to do some *research/argument* before buying a new computer.

6 The police are going to *wonder/investigate* the burglary.

7 We're getting a lot of *inquiries/question* about the new service.

8 It was a very interesting *debate/discuss* about immigration.

GRAMMAR QUESTION TAGS

4 Complete the questions with question tags.

1 We can walk there, _____?

2 They've already left, _____?

3 We'll see you later, _____?

4 You don't like jazz, _____?

5 The film was great, _____?

6 You spoke to Mr Johnston earlier, _____?

7 You won't need the car, _____?

8 You haven't lost your keys again, _____?

VOCABULARY PLUS WORD BUILDING: ADJECTIVES

5 Complete the words with the correct suffix.

1 His shoulder is very pain_____. He says it hurts a lot when he tries to move it.

2 Unfortunately, the number of home_____ people living on the streets has increased.

3 I'm afraid I'm not respons_____ for what happened. It wasn't my fault.

4 He's one of Japan's most creat_____ film directors. His work is very original and exciting.

5 The situation seemed hope_____. What we were trying to do was impossible.

6 It's a very effect_____ way to teach reading – we've had excellent results.

7 Don't worry about the car, I'm just thank_____ that nobody was hurt.

8 She was always a mess_____ child. She just loved getting dirty!

VOCABULARY PROBLEMS AND SOLUTIONS

6 Put the words in the correct order to make sentences.

1 car's / down / the / broken
_____

2 phone / recharging / my / needs
_____

3 out / it's / order / of
_____

4 printer / fixing / the / needs
_____

5 it / switching / off / try / and / again / on
_____

6 this / it / strange / making / noise / keeps
_____

7 more / work / doesn't / any / it
_____

8 out / have / it / we / sort / to
_____

FUNCTION MAKING AND RESPONDING TO POLITE REQUESTS

7 Underline the correct alternatives.

1 **A:** Could you *tell/to tell* me where I can find the manager?
   B: Yes, *of course/afraid*.
2 **A:** Do you know *if there's/if is there* a supermarket near here?
   B: I'm not *afraid/sure*.
3 **A:** Would you mind *checking/to check* the system for me?
   B: Of *course/sure* not.
4 **A:** Could you *see/to see* if anyone has arrived yet?
   B: Let me have a *look/course*.

VOCABULARY -ING/-ED ADJECTIVES

8 Complete the sentences with the correct form of the adjective in brackets.

1 Are you _____ with me just because I'm a bit late? (annoy)
2 There's a _____ atmosphere in the school. (relax)
3 It's all very _____. I can't understand the results of this survey. (confuse)
4 The hotel is lovely. She's _____ with the room even though it's small. (satisfy)
5 I realised I'd made a terrible mistake. It was so _____! (embarrass)
6 I was still _____ from the race. (exhaust)
7 You look _____. What's wrong? (worry)
8 It was a very _____ experience. (frighten)

GRAMMAR CONDITIONALS

9 A Underline the correct alternative.

1 If I have time later, *I call/I'll call* you.
2 If I *don't/wouldn't* sleep well enough, I feel terrible the next day.
3 If there *is/would be* anything else you need, just tell me.
4 Those plants *die/will die* unless you water them soon.
5 If we had more room, *I'll/I'd* invite them to stay.
6 It wouldn't be as bad if we *didn't/don't* have so many exams this year.
7 If I didn't have a car, I *will/would* cycle everywhere.
8 If we *won't/don't* leave now, we'll be late.
9 It's more expensive if you *live/lived* in a bigger house.
10 If we *get/will get* hungry, we'll buy some sandwiches.
11 She *would/will* get angry if we asked her.
12 Life would be easier if we *will have/had* more money.

B Circle the correct option to complete the sentences.

1 If it rains tonight, _____.
   a) I take an umbrella
   b) I'll stay at home and watch a DVD
   c) I don't go out
2 If Justine passes her exams, _____.
   a) her mother is delighted
   b) she has worked hard
   c) she'll go to university
3 If you eat too much junk food, _____.
   a) it's not good for your health
   b) you would be too fat
   c) you'll like pizza a lot
4 If I had a garden, _____.
   a) I'd grow my own vegetables
   b) I sit in the sun all day long
   c) I'll grow lots of beautiful flowers
5 When I'm bored _____.
   a) I'd watch the TV
   b) always I cook something to eat
   c) I usually read a book
6 _____ at the cinema if you want.
   a) I'm meeting you
   b) I'll meet you
   c) I'd meet you
7 _____, I'll meet you later.
   a) If I get all my work finished on time
   b) If I'll finish work on time
   c) When I'm finishing my work
8 He would look much better _____.
   a) when he'll buy some new clothes
   b) if he would sleep more
   c) if he cut his hair

VOCABULARY PLUS MULTI-WORD VERBS

10 Complete the sentences with *on, off, up* or *down*.

1 I couldn't believe it when my brother's friend tried to chat me _____.

2 It was an informal family barbecue, so she dressed _____ in old jeans and a T-shirt.

3 You just need to click _____ the icon to open the file.

4 Can I try these jeans _____, please?

5 When you've finished on the computer, can you log _____?

6 She enjoys spending time with her dad, but she doesn't get _____ with her mum very well.

7 I was so embarrassed when he took _____ his shoes in the theatre!

8 I want to settle _____ and have children one day.

9 I used to drink a lot of coffee, but recently I've gone _____ it.

10 If you scroll _____, you'll find a link right at the bottom of the page.

VOCABULARY VERB–NOUN COLLOCATIONS

11 Circle the correct option to complete the sentences.

1 They're _____ a plant sale in the village hall on Saturday.
  a) being   **b)** holding   **c)** doing

2 She's running a marathon to _____ money for cancer research.
  a) have   **b)** raise   **c)** do

3 They're _____ an experiment in bilingual education at my daughter's school.
  a) being   **b)** doing   **c)** having

4 If you get to the cinema early, can you _____ us some seats?
  a) have   **b)** put   **c)** get

5 Did you _____ that programme last night on killer whales?
  a) watch   **b)** seeing   **c)** look

6 How annoying. That man has just _____ the queue.
  a) held   **b)** walked   **c)** jumped

7 I think it's time I got my hair _____. It's far too long.
  a) wash   **b)** cut   **c)** dry

VOCABULARY LIFE EVENTS

12 Match 1–8 with a)–h) to make sentences.

1 She didn't stop at a red light
2 The relationship wasn't working
3 I got a place at university
4 He did very well in the interview
5 They want to live together
6 She was brilliant at the job
7 He had an accident on holiday
8 He lost his job at the factory

a) so I'm going to study psychology.
b) so she got promoted.
c) so she failed her driving test.
d) so he's looking for work.
e) so they split up.
f) so he had to fly home.
g) so they offered him the job.
h) so they've bought a house.

FUNCTION GIVING AND RESPONDING TO NEWS

13 Find and correct ten mistakes in the conversations.

Conversation 1
A: I'm sorry to have to telling you, but the train has been cancelled.
B: That annoying.

Conversation 2
A: I've got a good news for you.
B: What is it?
A: I've finished my painting.
B: Congratulation!

Conversation 3
A: There's something I've got to tell to you.
B: What?
A: I'm leaving San Francisco.
B: Oh. I'm sorry for hear that.

Conversation 4
A: You'll never guess to what.
B: What?
A: I got my promotion!
B: That's so fantastic news!

Conversation 5
A: Unfortunate, I didn't get the job.
B: That's real shame.

CHECK

Circle the correct option to complete the sentences.

1 Houses in the area have become much _____ recently.
   a) more affordable   **b)** more cheaper
   c) expensiver

2 People are able to work far _____ hours than before.
   a) most flexible   **b)** more flexible   **c)** the more flexible

3 The saxophone is _____ to learn than some other instruments.
   a) slightly the hard   **b)** slightly easy   **c)** slightly harder

4 Could you go and get the _____? I need to clean the floor.
   a) communications satellite   **b)** washing machine
   c) vacuum cleaner

5 Nowadays you can have a _____ to protect you from influenza.
   a) antibiotic   **b)** vaccination   **c)** genetic engineering

6 That's a very good _____.
   a) wonder   **b)** inquire   **c)** question

7 I'm doing _____ into how computers affect children.
   a) a research   **b)** some research   **c)** some investigate

8 You don't want to come with us, _____?
   a) would you   **b)** did you   **c)** do you

9 You've brought the camera with you, _____?
   a) did you   **b)** haven't you   **c)** didn't you

10 She _____ one of the best players in the world, isn't she?
   a) 's   **b)** will be   **c)** was

11 I couldn't do anything to make things better. I felt _____.
   a) effective   **b)** painful   **c)** useless

12 He's a very _____ puppy.
   a) lovable   **b)** creative   **c)** biological

13 My computer's _____. Can you help me?
   a) needs fixing   **b)** doesn't work   **c)** crashed

14 Could you tell me _____?
   a) what is the problem   **b)** what the problem is
   c) what the problem

15 Sure. Let me _____.
   a) look for   **b)** have a look   **c)** look at

16 I've had a really _____ week.
   a) exhausted   **b)** tired   **c)** exhausting

17 I get really _____ when he doesn't reply to my texts.
   a) annoyed   **b)** annoying   **c)** relaxed

18 I'll give you the present when _____ you.
   a) I will see   **b)** I would see   **c)** I see

19 If we can arrange everything, _____ to France for a holiday.
   a) we'll go   **b)** we go   **c)** we would go

20 _____ very tired when I have to travel a lot.
   a) I'll get   **b)** I get   **c)** I would get

21 It's a formal evening, so we must _____ in something nice.
   a) dress down   **b)** dress for   **c)** dress up

22 We're very different characters, but we _____ well.
   a) get off   **b)** get on   **c)** get on with

23 She's selling the paintings to _____ for charity.
   a) buy money   **b)** earn money   **c)** raise money

24 I'll get there early and get us some _____.
   a) seats   **b)** entrance   **c)** chair

25 If he _____ the drums late at night, I would sleep much better.
   a) doesn't play   **b)** didn't play   **c)** would play

26 Life _____ easier if we didn't have to work so hard.
   a) would be   **b)** is   **c)** was

27 I wouldn't mind if he _____ back again!
   a) always comes   **b)** never comes
   c) never came

28 She was _____ a job at their head office in Washington.
   a) offered to   **b)** offered   **c)** promoted

29 I'm really pleased _____ you that you've won first prize.
   a) tell   **b)** to tell   **c)** telling

30 **A:** Their house burned down in a fire.
   B: Oh no. That's _____.
   a) a shame   **b)** annoying   **c)** awful

RESULT   /30

7 SUCCESS

VOCABULARY

SUCCESS

1 Rewrite the second sentence so that it means the same as the first. Use the words in capitals and one other word.

1 She was born with an ability to play the piano. NATURAL

She has a _____natural talent_____ for playing the piano.

2 He needs to concentrate on what he is doing. FOCUS

He needs to _____ what he is doing.

3 She put a lot of effort into her maths project. HARD

She worked _____ her maths project.

4 He is one of the best tennis players from any country at the moment. WORLD

He's a _____ tennis player.

5 He's someone who is very successful. ACHIEVER

He's a _____.

6 It's important to think that you have the ability to do what you want. BELIEVE

It's important to _____ yourself.

READING

2 A Write down three tips you would give to someone starting their own business.

B Read the text. Does it mention your ideas?

MAKING IT HAPPEN

Women around the world setting up their own businesses may face sim kinds of barriers, despite the different contexts in which they live and work. But in spite of the problems they face, many have success storie to tell. We asked successful entrepreneurs for their tips for success.

BRIDGING TWO CULTURES

When Jiao Lee moved to Ireland from China, she saw the opportunity to start a business which could help to build bridges between the two countries she loved. She started China Tours as a small travel business, setting up tours between the two countries.

It was hard at first. She had to learn all about setting up a business in a foreign country and she struggled with language barriers. But it was all worth it. China Tours now employs more than forty people and has offices in Ireland and China. Jiao says, 'It has been such an exciting ride setting up China Tours and I've enjoyed every minute. I wouldn't want to work for anyone else now.'

Success Tip – Always keep an eye open for an opportunity. And don't be put off when things seem hard in the beginning. Stick with your ideas, and soon you will find success.

SWEET SUCCESS

When Carmen Spataro set up Sweet Dreams, a mobile cupcake business in her home city of Washington, she used social media to help spread the word about her new business. Travelling around the city in her pink van, selling her freshly-baked cupcakes, Carmen sends her followers updates on Facebook and Twitter, telling them where and when they can find the van. The idea has been a fantastic success, with customers sending each other messages about the new, delicious range of cakes on offer. 'I'm in cupcake heaven,' tweets one of her happy customers. 'I wasn't very confident with the technology at first,' says Carmen. 'But I learned quickly and now I love it. Using social media has helped to add to the sense of fun which we wanted to establish.'

Success Tip – Keep up-to-date with technology and use it to promote your business.

HATS OFF

Melissa Faith had no idea that her designs for children's hats would lead her to success in business.

She started by making a few hats to sell at a market. The hats were so popular that they sold out almost immediately. 'It was amazing. People were coming b for more and I couldn't keep up with the demand,' she explains. Melissa set up a website to sell t hats online. Loopy Kids HatZone was an instant success and Melis now exports hats all over the world. 'One of the problems I've had,' says Melissa, 'is that I'm dyslexic, so it's hard for me to ke up with all the paperwork and emailing.' However, she thinks th her dyslexia also helps her to be more creative and to have a fresh approach to problem-solving.

Success Tip – Be prepared for the unexpected. Some of the best things happ when you don't plan for them.

3 Read the text again and mark the statements T (true), F (false) or DK (don't know).

1 Jiao Lee had previous experience in the travel industry.
2 She found that language was a problem in the beginning.
3 Carmen was confident with new technology.
4 She sells her cakes around the city from a mobile van.
5 Melissa had always planned to start a company selling hats.
6 She finds it difficult to be creative at work.

4 Match words and phrases 1–6 from the text in Exercise 2 with definitions a)–f).

1 struggled with
2 barriers
3 (be) put off
4 spread the word
5 keep up with
6 a fresh approach to (something)

a) tell a lot of people about something
b) found it hard to do
c) make you not want to do something
d) a new way of looking at something
e) things that prevent you from doing something
f) do something as quickly as you need to

GRAMMAR

PRESENT PERFECT SIMPLE VERSUS CONTINUOUS

5 Complete the conversations with the present perfect simple or continuous form of the verbs in brackets. If both are possible, use the continuous form.

1 **A:** Your hair looks nice.
  B: Thank you. I _____ (go) to a new hairdresser. It's much cheaper.
2 **A:** Do you know what time the package is being delivered? I _____ (wait) all morning.
  B: I'll just check for you.
3 **A:** You look exhausted.
  B: I know. I _____ (not sleep) well recently.
4 **A:** Are you OK?
  B: Not really. The baby _____ (cry) all day. I don't know what to do.
5 **A:** Have you two met before?
  B: Yes, we _____ (know) each other since university.
6 **A:** You look well. Have you been away?
  B: Yes, we _____ (ski) in the Alps.
7 **A:** How long _____ they _____ (live) in Australia?
  B: For about five years. They moved there to be closer to his family.
8 **A:** _____ you _____ (watch) that new detective series?
  B: Yes, it's brilliant. I _____ really _____ (enjoy) it.

6 Complete the email with the present perfect simple or continuous form of the verbs in the box. If both are possible, use the continuous form.

not decide	find	not have	think	happen	look
work (x2)	study	stay			

Hi Nina,

How are you? Sorry I didn't write earlier, but so much
[1]_____ in the last few weeks,
I just [2]_____ any spare time.
Luke and Shauna [3]_____
with us. They were over from America, where Luke
[4]_____ on his new film. It was great
to see them and catch up on their news. Apparently, they
[5]_____ about moving back to Asia,
but they [6]_____ for sure yet.
Things over here are good. We [7]_____
for somewhere new to live. Our landlord wants
us to leave, which is a shame. But we might
[8]_____ somewhere near the
centre. It's a beautiful flat overlooking the river. And it's
only five minutes' walk from the restaurant where I
[9]_____ at weekends. So, that
would be fine. Jimmy [10]_____
hard for his exams – they're next month, so keep your
fingers crossed.
I'll write again soon. Take care of yourself.
Much love,
Kelly

VOCABULARY PLUS

VERB PHRASES

7 A Match verb phrases 1–8 with a preposition from the box.

on	about	for	to	in

1 depend _____
2 succeed _____
3 pay attention _____
4 rely _____
5 pick up _____
6 have a talent _____
7 think _____
8 have access _____

B Complete the sentences with a suitable phrase from Exercise 7A.

1 You don't have to decide straightaway. Why don't you _____ it for a while?
2 This is important. Try to _____ what the man is saying.
3 Both solutions could be right. It _____ your point of view.
4 I'd like to _____ something you said earlier.
5 You obviously _____ music. You play very well for a beginner.
6 We _____ thousands of books in the university library.
7 I'm not sure if they'll _____ winning the election, but it's a good campaign.
8 I can't _____ you to be there on time because you're usually late.

VOCABULARY

ABILITY

1 A Circle the correct options to complete the text.

Princess Diana

John Lennon

Schoolteachers may be experts ¹_____ their subjects, but they aren't always right about their students. Some of the most brilliant people in British history were ²_____ at school and got terrible reports. In his school report, John Lennon was described as '³_____ – certainly on the road to failure.' Winston Churchill, future Prime Minister and probably Britain's most ⁴_____ politician, clearly had a lot ⁵_____ as a student, but his behaviour was so bad that his teacher wrote, 'I really don't know what to do.' Stephen Fry's teacher didn't realise Fry had an ⁶_____ English. A fine actor, comedian and writer, Fry was bottom of his class. Robert Graves, a ⁷_____ schoolboy writer who became one of Britain's greatest poets, left school with this message from his headmaster, 'Well, goodbye, Graves and remember that your best friend is the wastepaper basket.' One of Diana, Princess of Wales's teachers was correct in that Diana wasn't a ⁸_____ student, but the teacher also wrote, interestingly, that she 'must try to be less emotional … with others.'

1 a) at	**b)** for	**c)** in
2 a) useless	**b)** useful	**c)** gifted
3 a) skilful	**b)** hopeless	**c)** an expert
4 a) useless	**b)** hopeless	**c)** skilful
5 a) of ability	**b)** of skilful	**c)** of talented
6 a) expert in	**b)** aptitude for	**c)** aptitude to
7 a) gifted	**b)** expert	**c)** talent in
8 a) gifted at	**b)** expert	**c)** talented

B Look at the words and phrases in the box and answer the questions.

gifted	have a lot of ability	have an aptitude for
expert	hopeless skilful	talented useless

1 Which two are negative? _____

2 Which two are adjectives that mean you are naturally very good at something? _____

3 Which is an adjective that means you are good at something (you practised it)?

_____

4 Which is a noun that describes someone who knows a lot about something? _____

5 Which two phrases mean you are naturally good at something? _____

GRAMMAR

PRESENT AND PAST ABILITY

2 Complete the text with the words in the box.

manage   managed   to   was   wasn't   remember
couldn't   could

THE REAL RAIN MAN

In 1989, actor Dustin Hoffman won an Oscar for his role in *Rain Man*. While accepting it, he said, 'My special thanks to Kim Peek for making *Rain Man* a reality.' But who was Kim Peek? Peek was a man with a mental disability, who ¹_____ do many simple things such as dressing himself, but could remember enormous amounts of information.

Peek didn't ²_____ to walk until he was four, but from the age of 16–20 months, he was able to ³_____ large amounts of information. As a teenager, he memorised whole books.

In later life, he ⁴_____ able to read a book in one hour and he remembered approximately 98.7 percent of everything he read. He ⁵_____ recite the content of around 12,000 books about history, geography, sports and many other subjects. He was also able ⁶_____ remember thousands of different pieces of music, though he ⁷_____ able to play them all because of his physical disability.

Kim travelled with his father all over the US and Canada, speaking about how he ⁸_____ to live a full life even though he was disabled. He died in 2009.

3 Cross out the alternative which is **not** possible.

1 We *didn't manage to/couldn't/didn't manage* speak to John this morning.

2 I *can/'m able to/do able to* speak five languages.

3 Ugo *managed to/could/was able to* finish the report yesterday.

4 Twenty years ago, I *was able to/can/could* run ten kilometres.

5 Few of us *can/are manage to/are able to* work without technology these days.

6 Women *didn't able to/weren't able to/couldn't* vote in Switzerland until 1971.

7 I *can't/'m not able to/'m not manage to* come to class tomorrow.

8 When we finished the work, we *were able to/could to/could* have a break.

9 *Are you able to/Do you can/Can you* write computer programmes?

10 *Did you manage/Were you able/Could you* to do your homework?

4 A Read the pairs of sentences aloud. Tick the pairs that have the same number of syllables.

1 **a)** He's very gifted.
  b) She's really skilful.
2 **a)** He has an aptitude for sport.
  b) I'm hopeless at gymnastics.
3 **a)** He thinks he's useless.
  b) She has a talent.
4 **a)** They say he's an expert.
  b) She has great ability.

B ▶ 7.1 Listen and shadow the sentences. Concentrate on the rhythm.

LISTENING

5 A Pictures A–F show moments in the life of a genius. What do you think is happening in each picture?

A seven months
B eighteen months — NEW YORK TIMES
C six years
D nine years
E DAILY NEWS — Fall of a genius
F WILLIAM SIDIS 1898–1944

B ▶ 7.2 Listen to William Sidis's story and check your answers.

C Listen again and answer the questions.

1 Where were his parents from originally, and where did they move to?
2 What was William's first word?
3 How old was William when he could speak Russian, French, German and Hebrew?
4 What did he do at Harvard University when he was nine?
5 What did he do two years later?
6 Who 'followed him around'?
7 What two things did his sister say about his ability to learn languages?
8 For most of his adult life, what was Sidis 'running away' from?

WRITING

A SUMMARY; LEARN TO MAKE NOTES FOR A SUMMARY

6 A Read the notes for a summary of the story in Exercise 5 and audio script 7.2 on page 78.

1 Find two mistakes in the notes.
2 Find two examples of places where the writer copied exact words.

THE LIFE OF WILLIAM SIDIS

Background
- Lived in New York
- Father: psychologist at Harvard (Russian roots)

Childhood
- Born 1898
- 6 months: could speak. First word = 'moon'.
- 18 months: read newspaper
- 3 years: could type
- As a child, spoke Russian, French, German & Hebrew
- As a child, gave maths lecture at Harvard Uni
- 11 yrs: attended Harvard Uni

Adulthood
- Wanted a quiet life
- Journalists followed him around and wrote articles about this young genius
- Didn't like fame
- 1944: died

Myths
- His sister = close 2 him & spoke about him after he died
- Knew all world's languages
- Took 1 week to learn a language
- IQ of 250–300

Conclusion
- Not all childhood geniuses will produce great things as adults
- Need to leave people alone to live their lives

B Which of the following are included in the notes? Tick the ones you find.

1 an abbreviation
2 a symbol for 'and'
3 a number to represent a word that sounds the same
4 a heading
5 a subheading
6 highlighted information

C Write a summary of the story (120–150 words) using the notes in Exercise 6A.

William Sidis is sometimes called 'the most intelligent man ever', but he isn't famous and his life was not full of great achievements. He was born …

VOCABULARY
QUALIFICATIONS

1 What are the people in 1–10 talking about? Choose from the words in the box.

> qualifications   a certificate   a degree   an MA
> a driving licence   an online course   a PhD
> face-to-face learning   distance learning
> an apprenticeship

1 I got my first degree in 2005 and always wanted to study the subject more deeply so I finally began one last year. _____

2 I much prefer it because I like to be with other students in the same room. That's how I learn best. _____

3 My brother did one in a fashion company. They were nice to him and they showed him the basics of the business. _____

4 I don't really have any because I left school when I was fourteen, but I worked hard and was a success. _____

5 Mine is framed and hanging on my wall! It's evidence that I took the one-month course and it was necessary for me to get a job. _____

6 You really need it to be a university professor. It's the hardest academic qualification and it involves original research, but it's necessary. _____

7 I did one once. It was interesting because you write lots of messages to the other students but you never meet them. I passed. _____

8 It's the way education has been going for a long time. It means people from isolated parts of the world can study at a good university even if they can't travel there. _____

9 It took me five attempts to get mine! The first time I tried, I crashed and the instructor just said, 'OK, come back next week!' _____

10 When I finish school I'd like to go to university to study history, so I hope I'll have one by the time I'm twenty-one or twenty-two. _____

FUNCTION
CLARIFYING OPINIONS

2 A ▶ 7.3 Listen to conversations 1–3. What is happening in each one? Circle the correct option to complete the sentences.

Conversation 1
Parents are discussing a child's _____.
a) behaviour
b) TV-watching habits
c) school grades

Conversation 2
Colleagues are discussing _____.
a) another colleague's work
b) their qualifications
c) the best person for a job

Conversation 3
A presenter is asking a question about _____.
a) directing a play in a school theatre
b) the government's view of education
c) lack of money for the arts in schools

B Listen again. Which sentence do you hear, a) or b)?

Conversation 1
1 a) In my view, it's getting out of control.
  b) For my view, it's getting out of control.
2 a) By example, she watched TV for six hours yesterday.
  b) For example, she watched TV for six hours yesterday.
3 a) I'm saying that's a lot.
  b) I must say that's a lot.
4 a) That's not what I'm saying. She's always in front of a screen.
  b) That's what I was saying. She's always in front of a screen.

Conversation 2
5 a) For me, Elizabeth is the best.
  b) To me, Elizabeth is the best.
6 a) For once, she has the right qualifications.
  b) For one thing, she has the right qualifications.
7 a) She would, but now I've said that, she already has a good job.
  b) She would, but having said that, she already has a good job.

Conversation 3
8 a) Yes, the reason I say this is that funding has been cut for arts subjects.
  b) Yes, it's reasonable to say that funding has been cut for arts subjects.
9 a) Let me give you an example. A school I visited last month wanted to do a play in the little school theatre.
  b) Let's look at the example. A school I visited last month wanted to do a play in the little school theatre.
10 a) Like I'm saying, money isn't everything, but it's part of the problem.
  b) Like I said, money isn't everything, but it's part of the problem.

VOCABULARY

GETTING ON

1 Put the pairs of words in the box into the correct places in sentences 1–10 below.

on my	us over	~~on well~~	my own	
disturb me	friends with	to myself		
a nuisance	nosy about	to know		

on well

1 Joachim gets ⟨ with his mother but he's always arguing with his father.

2 I am really interested in other people – actually my mum says I am too other people's lives.

3 Whenever they're arguing, I prefer to mind business. I don't get involved.

4 Hayley has invited for dinner at her house. Can we go?

5 Those neighbours are – they're always playing loud music and making a mess.

6 She got her neighbours immediately. They were really friendly and chatty.

7 Please don't. I'm trying to do some work.

8 One thing that gets nerves is when the neighbours have noisy parties!

9 Xun hasn't made her neighbours yet but she only moved in last week.

10 I keep myself. I hate chatting about nothing – it's a waste of time.

GRAMMAR

ARTICLES AND QUANTIFIERS

2 Add *a*, *an* or *the* where necessary.

a

1 Do you want ⟨ drink?

2 Have you received letter I sent you?

3 Dogs are wonderful pets.

4 Do you have pen I can borrow?

5 She went to Paris on Wednesday.

6 Is there airport in the city?

7 I'm going to Germany in morning.

8 We live by Pacific Ocean.

9 My brother is actor.

10 Nurses aren't paid enough.

11 He doesn't have children.

12 Did you see film I told you about?

13 I live in United States.

14 She's nicest woman I know.

15 Do you like apples?

3 Make sentences with one word or phrase from each section.

1	~~We went there for a~~	a)	of us love this	i)	of friends in this community.
2	There are plenty	b)	of good restaurants in the town,	ii)	in Poland when I was younger.
3	I don't know	c)	many cars in most	iii)	I like the architecture.
4	All	d)	~~few days in~~	iv)	~~June last year.~~
5	If you have enough	e)	lots	v)	place because it's so friendly.
6	There are too	f)	much about this city, but	vi)	especially if you like French food.
7	I've got	g)	time, go	vii)	to the museum – it's great.
8	I spent a bit	h)	of time	viii)	big cities – I hate traffic!

1 *We went there for a few days in June last year.*

2 _____

3 _____

4 _____

5 _____

6 _____

7 _____

8 _____

4 Read the text. Which lines are correct? Which have an extra word?

In the past, a small English village called t̶h̶e̶ Lanreath, in Cornwall, had three pubs, two shops and a post office. Now it doesn't have but any of these. The post office, the last shop and the last pub were all of recently closed down. Now the council wants to close the primary school. The school has had excellent results and is very popular with children and parents. The problem is that the school doesn't have enough students and the council says it costs too much to money to keep it open for only a small few children. The villagers decided to fight the council's ruling. The whole village packed up, including sheep and cows, and travelled a five hours to London. They went to a park and created a miniature Lanreath. They showed the more best of village life – playing traditional games, doing a traditional dance and holding a cake sale. Some of all the teachers also taught a lesson for Lanreath Primary School pupils.

The BBC made a TV programme about the story: *Power To The People: The Invasion of Islington*, presented by a Tim Samuels.

1	*the*
2	✓
3	_____
4	_____
5	_____
6	_____
7	_____
8	_____
9	_____
10	_____
11	_____
12	_____
13	_____
14	_____
15	_____
16	_____
17	_____

LISTENING

5 A ▶ 8.1 **Listen to interviews with Elise and Marc about neighbours and answer the questions for each person.**

1 Who are their neighbours?
   Elise: _____
   Marc: _____
2 Why do they like the situation with their neighbours?
   Elise: _____
   Marc: _____
3 How often do they see their neighbours?
   Elise: _____
   Marc: _____
4 How long have the people lived there?
   Elise: _____
   Marc: _____

B **Complete the summaries with one word in each space. Then listen again and check.**

> Elise says she has the [1]_____ neighbours. She sees them a lot because she works in the [2]_____ business. Her extended family consists of [3]_____ people. They eat together every [4]_____. She thinks this situation is [5]_____ in many countries. She has never asked her [6]_____ if he likes living so close to her family.

> Marc's nearest neighbours are two cows that live [7]_____ miles away! Marc and his wife used to live in [8]_____, but they didn't like the crowds, the noise and using public [9]_____. They bought a [10]_____ ten years ago. Marc and his wife work [11]_____. Marc says the interviewer is the [12]_____ person they've seen this year!

C **Circle the best alternative way of saying these extracts from the interviews.**

1 If I need a babysitter for my kids …
   a) If I need someone to look after my children …
   b) If my children need to sit still …
2 You never get fed up with the family?
   a) You never eat with the family?
   b) You never get tired of the family?
3 We always wanted to live side by side.
   a) We always wanted to live in the same town.
   b) We always wanted to live next to each other.
4 We really are completely isolated.
   a) We really like to be close to nature.
   b) There are no other people near us.
5 It's not a functioning farm.
   a) The farm doesn't make much money.
   b) The place isn't actually used as a farm.
6 We're a bit antisocial.
   a) We don't like mixing with other people.
   b) We don't like working for big companies.

VOCABULARY PLUS

COMPOUND NOUNS

6 A **Match the words in box A with the words in box B to make compound nouns.**

A

> ~~traffic~~ high housing sports industrial car super language shopping one-way terraced outdoor gift primary

B

> houses ~~lights~~ shop school (×2) centre (×2) street (×2) park market (×2) estate (×2)

1	_traffic lights_	8	_____
2	_____	9	_____
3	_____	10	_____
4	_____	11	_____
5	_____	12	_____
6	_____	13	_____
7	_____	14	_____

B ▶ 8.2 **Listen and check. Then listen and repeat. Concentrate on the stress patterns.**

7 **Complete the sentences with a compound noun from Exercise 6A.**

1 My best friend lives in a house on a big new _____ in Bristol.
2 I'm studying English for six weeks in a _____ in Bath.
3 My son will be old enough to go to _____ next year.
4 You can't drive your car down there – it's a _____!
5 I use the gym in the _____.
6 We live in a row of small _____ in Barton Road.
7 Drive along the High Street and turn left at the _____.
8 We left the car in the _____ while we went shopping.
9 I buy my food in the _____ because it's more convenient than going to lots of small shops.
10 There's a _____ in the art gallery where you can buy postcards of some of the paintings.
11 Our town has an _____ every Thursday behind the bus station – I buy all my vegetables there.
12 Ben's new company has an office on an _____ just outside Coventry.
13 There's an internet café in the _____, between the cinema and the book shop.
14 My daughter and her friends spend most Saturdays in the _____, although I don't think they buy much!

VOCABULARY
THE INTERNET

1 Read the situations and write the type of website or web page a)–l) the speakers need.

1 'I want to write my day-to-day thoughts and publish them on the internet.' ___blog___
2 'I need my own website that tells people who I am and what I do.' _____
3 'I just need to find some information very quickly.' _____
4 'I'm looking for love.' _____
5 'I want to put my photos on the net so my friends and family can see them.' _____
6 'I need some information about a big company that I might work for.' _____
7 'I want to find out what's going on in the world.' _____
8 'I want to make new friends and find out what my old friends are doing.' _____
9 'I want to find out the best places to go for a holiday.' _____
10 'I'd like to read short reviews of films, restaurants, etc., to see which are the best.' _____
11 'I'd like to see this film clip that my friend uploaded onto the net.' _____
12 'I want to write an online encyclopedia that everyone can contribute to.' _____

a) blog
b) photo sharing site
c) ratings site
d) video sharing site
e) social networking site
f) search engine
g) wiki
h) travel site
i) news site
j) personal homepage
k) dating site
l) corporate website

GRAMMAR
RELATIVE CLAUSES

2 Match each pair of sentences with the correct explanation, a) or b).

1 The children, who love films, went to the cinema. *b*
2 The children who love films went to the cinema. *a*
   a) Only some of the children went to the cinema.
   b) All of the children went to the cinema.
3 Her brother, who is a musician, lives in New York.
4 Her brother who is a musician lives in New York.
   a) She has one brother. He lives in New York.
   b) She has more than one brother. One of them lives in New York.

5 My house, which is by the beach, has a great view.
6 My house which is by the beach has a great view.
   a) I have more than one house.
   b) I have only one house.
7 They went to the only school in the village, which had good teachers.
8 They went to the only school in the village which had good teachers.
   a) There was more than one school in the village, but only one had good teachers.
   b) There was only one school in the village.

3 Complete the quotations of definitions with the words in the box.

| thing that | who behaves | clothing that | which has |
| person who | place where | name that | a place |

1 'A jumper is an item of _____ is worn by a child when his or her mother is cold.'
2 'A dictionary is the only _____ success comes before work.'
3 'A coward is a _____, when faced with danger, thinks with his feet.'
4 'Experience is the _____ men give to their mistakes.'
5 'A cigarette is a bit of tobacco in paper _____ fire at one end and an idiot at the other.'
6 'An advertisement is a _____ persuades you to spend money you don't have on things you don't need.'
7 'A babysitter is a teenager _____ like an adult so adults can behave like teenagers.'
8 'A bank is a _____ you keep the government's money in your name.'

4 ▶ 8.3 Listen for the pauses where there are commas. Tick the sentence you hear.

1 a) The website which we built is too slow.
   b) The website, which we built, is too slow.
2 a) Those people who are always working don't enjoy life.
   b) Those people, who are always working, don't enjoy life.
3 a) The ratings site which I check every day is growing fast.
   b) The ratings site, which I check every day, is growing fast.
4 a) Those students who do online courses love studying.
   b) Those students, who do online courses, love studying.
5 a) Near my flat where you're staying there's a supermarket.
   b) Near my flat, where you're staying, there's a supermarket.

READING

5 A Look at the picture and the title of the text below. What do you think a *silver surfer* is?

B Read the text and answer the questions.

1 Who introduced Barbara to the internet?

_____

2 Why did Barbara dislike it at first?

_____

3 What age are most of the people who go online?

_____

4 Why did Barbara feel lonely before she used the internet?

_____

5 Which type of online communication do silver surfers use the most?

_____

C Match words 1–5 from the text with definitions a)–e).

1 to adapt (paragraph 1)

2 to take to it (paragraph 2)

3 absolutely (paragraph 2)

4 the majority (paragraph 3)

5 avid (paragraph 5)

a) to start doing something new as a habit

b) the larger number or part of something

c) completely

d) very keen or interested

e) to change something to fit a different situation

WRITING

A WEBSITE REVIEW; LEARN TO USE COMPLEX SENTENCES

6 A Complete gaps 1–4 in paragraphs A–D with the words in the box.

> like   feature   best   would

A ☐ Another [1]_____ I like is the book reviews. Regular users of the website often write these. Even though the writers aren't professionals, some of the reviews are excellent and they give you a good idea of what's in the book.

B ☐ One website I really [2]_____ is amazon.com. It is a website for buying books. One reason I'd recommend it is because you can buy used books. This means you can get really good books for half the price they cost in the shops.

C ☐ Finally, I [3]_____ recommend this website to anybody who is interested in books. Even if you don't buy anything, it is fun to surf the site, and a great source of information about books of all types.

D ☐ The [4]_____ thing about Amazon, though, is the fact that it is so easy to use and you can trust it. I have ordered dozens of books through Amazon and the books have always arrived quickly and in good condition.

B Put the paragraphs of the website review in the correct order.

C Write a website review (120–150 words).

/////SILVER SURFERS/////

1 When Sonya Alanis showed her grandmother, Barbara, how to use a few online tools, she didn't really think her older relative would be very interested. But two years later she is amazed at how well her grandmother has adapted to the world of the internet. Barbara now has her own online profile, does her shopping online and is in regular contact with her granddaughter using live chat and email. And she isn't showing any signs of stopping.

2 'I was using my tablet one day,' explained Sonya, 'and my grandmother asked me what I was spending so much time doing. She found it quite annoying I think, mostly because she didn't really understand it. So I showed her some of the things I use – social networking, online chat, that kind of thing. I didn't really think she would take to it at all but she absolutely loved it. Now I'm at university and she messages me every day. I think she is online more than me to be honest.'

3 Barbara has become a silver surfer and she's not alone. In the last few years, the world of the internet has grown up. Although people below the age of 50 still make up the majority of internet users, older people are logging on in larger and larger numbers. And once they've started, the internet becomes an everyday part of their lives.

4 Barbara has some ideas about why this change has happened. 'Once I learnt how to surf and message people it changed my life', she said. 'Before the internet I was quite lonely. My family are wonderful but they live quite far away and they are all so busy. I don't drive so I can't visit them very easily – in fact I usually only go out when they have time to take me. I use public transport occasionally but I find it difficult to  carry large bags of shopping or to find my way around busy towns. So using the internet makes my life much easier. I can contact people every day and I keep in touch with people more easily.'

5 Once older people find that using the internet is so convenient, they often become avid users, though in a different way to young people. Silver surfers use email the most, sending messages to share information and contact family and friends. They also use the internet to find health information and to book travel tickets or shop online. As Sonya says, 'My grandmother is now giving me advice on new apps! She's getting better at using the web than me!'

VOCABULARY
WELCOMING

1 A Make phrases for welcoming with the words in the boxes. Then complete the conversations.

| at mess make the yourself help home excuse yourself |

1 A: Can I try one of these cakes?
B: Yes, _____.
2 A: Come in. _____.
B: It looks very tidy to me. You should see my place!
3 A: Welcome! _____.
B: Thanks. What a nice room.

| my seat up guest put a be your have feet |

4 A: May I use your phone, please?
B: _____.
5 A: Good morning. I'm here to see Mr Drucker.
B: I'll tell him you're here. _____.
6 A: You must be exhausted. _____.
B: Thank you. Yes, it was a really tiring day.

B Match pictures A–F with the conversations in Exercise 1A.

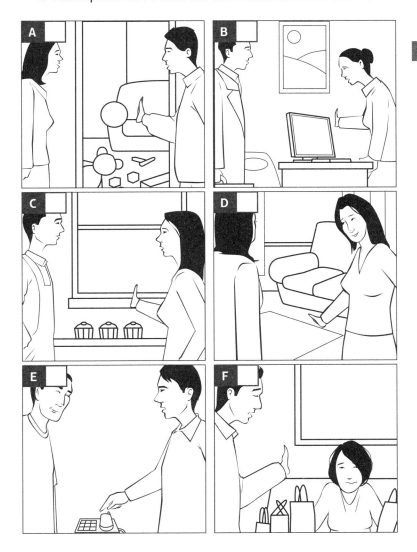

FUNCTION
BEING A GOOD GUEST

2 Tick the correct sentences.
1 a) Is it OK if I arrive half an hour late?
b) Is it OK if I'm arrive half an hour late?
2 a) What we should do if we get lost?
b) What should we do if we get lost?
3 a) Do I need to bring a present?
b) Do I need bring a present?
4 a) Was I did something wrong?
b) Did I do something wrong?
5 a) Is this a bad time? I come back later.
b) Is this a bad time? I can come back later.
6 a) If I'm you, I'd apologise.
b) If I were you, I'd apologise.
7 a) Sorry about that. I didn't know.
b) Sorry for that. I didn't know.
8 a) My apologise. I didn't realise.
b) My apologies. I didn't realise.
9 a) No, it's not the necessary.
b) No, it's not necessary.
10 a) Don't worry. It's fine.
b) You don't worry. It's fine.

LEARN TO
ACCEPT APOLOGIES

3 Underline the correct alternative.
1 A: I'm really sorry. I broke this cup.
B: *It's no problem./It's not the problem.*
2 A: Sorry, I didn't phone you before coming. I can see you're busy.
B: *Not at all./Not all.* I'll be finished in just a minute.
3 A: My apologies. I didn't realise you were working.
B: *That's too right./That's all right.* I'm not doing anything important.
4 A: Sorry, did I do something wrong? I didn't know I had to shake everyone's hand.
B: *It's very fine./It's fine.* I don't think anyone noticed.
5 A: I forgot to send you the notes from the last meeting. Sorry about that.
B: *Nothing./It's nothing.* Don't worry about it.
6 A: I'm sorry. I didn't bring anything for the children.
B: *You really don't have to./You really haven't to.* They're just happy to see you.

VOCABULARY SUCCESS

1 Tick two correct sentences. Correct the wrong sentences.

1 Our company focuses at quality software.
2 I had the opportunity to travel a lot last year.
3 It's important that we work hardly at this.
4 The key is to believe of yourself.
5 He's certainly a high achiever.
6 We'll improve if we are practise every day.

GRAMMAR PRESENT PERFECT SIMPLE VERSUS CONTINUOUS

2 Underline the correct alternative.

1 How long have you *known/been knowing* David?
2 She's angry – she's *waited/been waiting* for an hour!
3 This morning I've *read/been reading* a book called *Infinite Jest* – it's over a thousand pages long!
4 How many people have you *invited/been inviting* to this party?
5 My hands are dirty, I've *worked/been working* on the car.
6 For the last six years I've *learned/been learning* Arabic, but it's really difficult.
7 They don't want to rent *The Hunger Games* because they've *seen/been seeing* it already.
8 Hello. I don't think we've *met/been meeting* before.

VOCABULARY PLUS VERB PHRASES

3 Complete the text with the correct prepositions.

TOP BLOGGERS

The best bloggers pay attention ¹_____ what's going on in the world. They listen ²_____ influential people, pick up ³_____ the stories in the air and put ⁴_____ hours reading websites and doing their research. They don't just wait ⁵_____ the big stories; they find them in the corners where other people aren't looking. Of course, they rely ⁶_____ traditional media such as newspapers. All bloggers depend ⁷_____ other sources for their content, but they think ⁸_____ the issues and, rather than just agreeing ⁹_____ the journalists, they look ¹⁰_____ alternative opinions. Often the best bloggers belong ¹¹_____ groups or societies that have access ¹²_____ interesting people, so the bloggers can hear different opinions. The most important qualities for someone to succeed ¹³_____ the 'blogosphere' are to have a talent ¹⁴_____ writing and to believe ¹⁵_____ yourself. In this sense, they have a lot in common ¹⁶_____ traditional journalists, but bloggers don't have to worry ¹⁷_____ newspaper deadlines. The negative side? Bloggers usually don't get paid ¹⁸_____ their work.

VOCABULARY ABILITY

4 Put the words in the correct order to make answers to the questions.

1 **A:** Why do you think they asked him to write the textbook?
   B: subject / because / expert / he's / his / an / in
   _____

2 **A:** Why do you think he'll pass the exam?
   B: of / he / maths / because / lot / ability / has / in / a
   _____

3 **A:** Why do you think she'll become an Olympic gymnast?
   B: sport / she's / the / at / gifted / because
   _____

4 **A:** Why do you think they'll do well in Hollywood?
   B: talent / have / writing / because / a / scripts / for / they
   _____

5 **A:** Why do you think he'll become a professional golfer?
   B: aptitude / the / has / an / because / game / for / he
   _____

6 **A:** Why do you think you'll fail the test?
   B: science / at / absolutely / because / hopeless / I'm
   _____

GRAMMAR PRESENT AND PAST ABILITY

5 Rewrite the second sentence so that it means the same as the first. Use the words in capitals. Write three words. Contractions are one word.

1 We don't know how to play cards. CAN'T
   _____ cards.

2 She is a wonderful singer. CAN
   _____ really well.

3 Can you bring some drinks to the party? ABLE
   _____ to bring some drinks to the party?

4 We didn't have time to visit Las Vegas. MANAGE
   We _____ visit Las Vegas.

5 I failed the test. ABLE
   I _____ pass the test.

6 I can usually clean the house in about two hours. MANAGE
   I usually _____ the house in about two hours.

7 What languages were you able to speak when you were a child? COULD
   What languages _____ when you were a child?

8 They succeeded in breaking the record. MANAGED
   They _____ the record.

VOCABULARY QUALIFICATIONS

6 Complete the text with the words in the box.

> Master's   apprenticeship   licence   distance
> qualifications   online   degree   learning

When I left school, I had no [1]_____ except my driving [2]_____. I needed that because I spent most of my time in stolen cars. When I was eighteen, a friend of my father's told me I could do an [3]_____ in his printing company, but because I couldn't read or write, I refused. Instead, I got involved in serious crime. Aged nineteen, I was sent to prison. This was my first taste of real education. Although there was no formal face-to-face [4]_____, one of the inmates taught me to read and write. Later, he told me about [5]_____ learning. We were allowed access to computers for a few hours a week, so I started an [6]_____ course. After three years, I got a [7]_____ in psychology. It was the best day of my life. When I left prison, I went on to do a [8]_____ and I became a youth worker, advising young people how to avoid a life of crime.

FUNCTION CLARIFYING OPINIONS; REFERRING TO WHAT YOU SAID EARLIER

7 A Underline the correct alternatives.

A: In my [1]*views/view*, sport is wonderful. The [2]*reasoning/reason* I say this is that it makes people work in teams. [3]*For/To* me, that's really important.

B: I [4]*can/must* say I agree with you. [5]*And/For* one thing, it keeps you healthy. For [6]*another/other*, it's good for your character. [7]*For/In* example, you learn teamwork.

A: That's [8]*it/what* I was saying: you learn to work together And like I [9]*told/said*, it's also good for your health.

B: That's right. I [10]*will/do* think children should play more sport in school.

A: And they can join clubs, too. Let me [11]*do/give* you an example: my kids are in an after-school athletics club.

B: That's great. Having [12]*said/spoken* that, those clubs can be very expensive.

B Which of the expressions 1–12 in Exercise 7A are for giving opinions (O)? Which are for giving examples (E)? Which are for referring to what you said earlier (R)?

1 _____	7 _____
2 _____	8 _____
3 _____	9 _____
4 _____	10 _____
5 _____	11 _____
6 _____	12 _____

VOCABULARY GETTING ON

8 Put the letters in brackets in the correct order to make a word. Then rewrite the sentences using that word and <u>two</u> other words.

1 That music is really annoying. (revesn)
That music really gets *on my nerves* .

2 I don't like mixing with other people. (mlseyf)
I prefer to keep _____.

3 She spent time finding out a lot about me. (gto)
She _____ me well.

4 Why don't you stop interfering in my life? (binesssu)
Why don't you mind _____?

5 They asked us to have dinner with them. (orev)
They invited us _____.

6 I have a great relationship with my dad. (lwle)
My dad and I _____.

GRAMMAR ARTICLES AND QUANTIFIERS

9 Are the two underlined parts of the sentences correct? Change the ones that are wrong.

1 I went to school in <u>a small town</u> in ✓ / <u>United States</u>.   *the*

2 My cousin, who is from <u>the West Indies</u>, is <u>an architect</u>.

3 <u>Golf players</u> don't usually make much money, but <u>best ones</u> are millionaires.

4 We saw <u>a rat</u>. The next day our cat killed <u>rat</u>.

5 I didn't enjoy <u>a party</u> – there were <u>too much people</u>.

6 Do you know <u>any good hairdressers</u>? I need <u>the haircut</u>.

7 <u>Plenty of people</u> would happily pay to travel to <u>moon</u>.

8 I need an MA, but it takes <u>too many time</u> and I don't have <u>enough money</u>.

9 To finish the dish, add <u>a little salt</u> and <u>lot of pepper</u>.

10 <u>Some of us</u> are planning to go to <u>the Barcelona</u> this weekend.

VOCABULARY PLUS COMPOUND NOUNS

10 Cross out the word which does not belong.

1 jam / traffic / lights / ~~person~~

2 car / park / house / rental

3 calling / gift / duty-free / shop

4 industrial / school / housing / estate

5 apartment / primary / language / school

6 one-way / high / news / street

7 shopping / mall / shops / centre

8 semi-detached / flat / terraced / houses

VOCABULARY THE INTERNET

11 Tick six correct sentences. Correct the wrong sentences.

       Wikis

1 ~~Blogs~~ ✓ are mini-encyclopedias containing useful information.
2 We use search engines to find information quickly.
3 Dating sites contain information about companies and businesses.
4 Wikis tell us which products, films, places, etc. are the best.
5 Photo sharing sites let us upload our pictures so our friends can see them.
6 Ratings sites tell us about individuals – their family, friends and hobbies, etc.
7 News sites tell us what's happening in the world.
8 Social networking sites let us stay in contact with old friends and make new ones.
9 Travel sites allow us to research places and sometimes book holidays.
10 We use personal homepages to find a partner.
11 Video sharing sites allow people to put film clips on the web.
12 Corporate websites are a type of online journal.

GRAMMAR RELATIVE CLAUSES

12 Join the sentences using *which*, *where* or *who*.

1 I spoke to a doctor. He was very nice.
  The doctor _____.
2 We visited a museum. It had a wonderful exhibition.
  The museum _____.
3 She was born on an island. It's now under water.
  The island _____.
4 My girlfriend is in the fashion industry. She lives in Paris.
  My girlfriend, _____.
5 I grew up in a house. It's now a theatre.
  The house _____.
6 Tom is my best friend. He works with my father.
  Tom, _____.
7 The sale in Macy's lasted for ten days. It's now finished.
  The sale in Macy's, _____.

VOCABULARY WELCOMING

13 Complete the sentences with a suitable verb.

1 Welcome to the company. Please _____ a seat.
2 You want to use the phone? _____ my guest.
3 Come in. _____ the mess. I've been very busy.
4 Let me take your coat. _____ yourself at home.
5 You look tired. Why don't you _____ your feet up?
6 Hungry? Please _____ yourself.

FUNCTION BEING A GOOD GUEST

14 Read the conversations. Cross out ten extra words.

Conversation 1

Pete: Hi, Don. Is it OK if I ~~to~~ bring a friend to your party?
Don: Yes, of course. No problem.
Pete: Oh, and one other thing. Do I need for to bring anything?
Don: No, it's not the necessary. We have everything we need.

Conversation 2

Joe: I put my feet on the table. Did I do something wrong?
Kat: Oh. It's considered be a bit rude.
Joe: Really? Sorry about that. I didn't know.
Kat: It's OK – we can explain you didn't understand.

Conversation 3

Andre: Is this for a bad time? I can come back later.
Bella: Can you to come back in ten minutes?
Andre: Yes, of course. My apologies. I didn't can realise you were in a meeting.
Bella: It's fine. Don't to worry about it.

Conversation 4

Nick: We caught Roger stealing again. What should we to do?
Tam: If I were you, I'd give him a final warning. You haven't told anyone else?
Nick: No, of course not. OK, I'll do that. Should I tell my boss?
Tam: No, you'd better be not.

LEARN TO ACCEPT APOLOGIES

15 Add the words in the box to the correct place in B's replies in the conversations.

all right   it's (×2)   no   at   ~~to~~

1 **A:** Sorry I didn't bring a dish. I just didn't have time.
                         to
  B: You really don't have ✓ apologise. We weren't expecting anything!
2 **A:** I'm sorry – I forgot to bring my notes.
  B: It's problem. I can photocopy mine.
3 **A:** Sorry, did I bump you?
  B: That's. It didn't hurt.
4 **A:** Sorry, am I late?
  B: Not all. We usually don't start till 3.15.
5 **A:** Sorry, did I step on your toe?
  B: No, nothing. I didn't even feel it.
6 **A:** I'm so sorry about missing lunch.
  B: Honestly, fine. Don't worry about it.

CHECK

Circle the correct option to complete the sentences.

1 We're going to focus _____ quality.
   a) to   b) on   c) by

2 For the last two hours _____ in the garden, so I'm tired.
   a) I'm working   b) I work   c) I've been working

3 June and I _____ each other for ten years.
   a) have been knowing   b) have known   c) are knowing

4 I think I like the new flat, but I _____ there long.
   a) haven't been living   b) 'm not living
   c) don't live

5 Bad news – his dog _____.
   a) is died   b) has been dying   c) has died

6 We really depend _____ our sponsors.
   a) of   b) to   c) on

7 You have _____ for tennis.
   a) an expert   b) an attitude   c) an aptitude

8 I'm hopeless _____ languages.
   a) in   b) on   c) at

9 Will you _____ finish your work on time?
   a) can   b) be able   c) manage to

10 I'm afraid I _____ to help you.
   a) 'm unable   b) can't   c) manage

11 When he was three, he _____ already talk.
   a) managed   b) was able   c) could

12 I'm _____ an apprenticeship in an internet company.
   a) doing   b) making   c) working

13 She's just got her driving _____.
   a) exam   b) licence   c) certificate

14 In my _____, Tokyo's the world's greatest city.
   a) view   b) opinions   c) thinking

15 Let me _____ you an example of what I mean.
   a) make   b) take   c) give

16 Those people should _____ their own business.
   a) take   b) mind   c) think

17 He's training to become _____.
   a) pilot   b) the pilot   c) a pilot

18 _____ usually start to walk at about twelve months.
   a) Children   b) The children   c) A child

19 There were _____ people at the party.
   a) plenty of   b) a few of   c) lots

20 I ate _____ ice cream and now I feel sick.
   a) too   b) too much   c) too many

21 We grew up on a _____ estate.
   a) housing   b) house   c) living

22 I often use search _____ to find out information.
   a) machines   b) engines   c) sites

23 I use a video _____ site.
   a) internet   b) loading   c) sharing

24 The road _____ we wanted to take was closed.
   a) that   b) where   c) what

25 Tillie, _____ is already at university.
   a) that's only sixteen,   b) who's only sixteen
   c) who's only sixteen,

26 The town _____ is full of trees.
   a) where I live   b) which I live   c) where, I live

27 Russia, _____ has changed a lot.
   a) which we visited in 1989,   b) which we visited in 1989   c) what we visited in 1989,

28 Come in and _____ yourself at home.
   a) be   b) take   c) make

29 My _____. I didn't know you were busy.
   a) disgrace   b) sorry   c) apologies

30 If this is a bad _____, I can come back later.
   a) time   b) hour   c) timing

RESULT	/30

9 HISTORY

VOCABULARY

HISTORY

1 A Find nouns in the word square that match meanings 1–10.

1 A complete change either in the way people think or in a country's political system
2 The time when an important change begins to happen (two words)
3 An event that changes a situation, or the process of growing or changing
4 When something increases and affects more people
5 Any change, discovery or invention that makes the world better
6 A group of people that works to achieve an aim
7 A machine, tool, system, etc., made for the first time
8 The basic idea or principle behind something
9 Something that someone learns about when it was not known before
10 Change that improves something

T	U	R	N	I	N	G	P	O	I	N	T
D	A	E	B	P	R	O	G	R	E	S	S
E	C	V	D	E	R	I	O	M	E	I	P
V	F	O	U	N	D	A	T	I	O	N	T
E	E	L	U	F	C	S	S	G	J	V	E
L	S	U	A	V	U	A	P	L	I	E	D
O	W	T	V	A	P	D	R	A	G	N	E
P	D	I	S	C	O	V	E	R	Y	T	X
M	E	O	R	E	K	A	A	E	I	I	H
E	D	N	I	U	F	N	D	O	E	O	O
N	C	I	N	T	I	C	F	R	S	N	E
T	M	O	V	E	M	E	N	T	C	L	F

B Underline the correct alternative.

1 History books say Alexander Fleming was responsible for the *foundation/discovery* of penicillin.
2 The internet has helped the *turning point/spread* of their ideas.
3 After finishing the research, we'll begin work on the *development/advance* of the product.
4 James is making a lot of *progress/discovery* in all his school subjects.
5 There have been amazing *advances/spreads* in technology in the last few years.
6 She was a member of the early feminist *progress/movement*.
7 Only a *foundation/revolution* will destroy this government.
8 I think the wheel is the greatest *invention/movement* in history.

GRAMMAR

HYPOTHETICAL CONDITIONAL: PAST

2 Circle the correct option to complete the sentences.

1 They would have said something if we _____ the rules.
   a) were broken **b)** would have broken
   c) had broken
2 If _____ you, I would have said 'hello'.
   a) I'd see **b)** I've seen
   c) I'd seen
3 He _____ if the ambulance hadn't come.
   a) would died **b)** would have died
   c) would have been died
4 If I'd known a ticket cost €100, I _____.
   a) wouldn't have come **b)** would have came
   c) not would have come
5 If the government hadn't lent the company a million pounds, it _____.
   a) had closed **b)** would close
   c) would have closed
6 They would have had a picnic if it _____.
   a) hadn't rained **b)** had rained not
   c) had been rained

3 Write a sentence with *if* for situations 1–6.

1 Early travellers invented boats. Cross-continental travel became possible.
   If early travellers hadn't invented boats, cross-continental travel wouldn't have become possible.
2 Archduke Ferdinand was assassinated. World War I started.
   _____
3 People from Sumer needed permanent records. They invented writing.
   _____
4 William the Conqueror invaded England in 1066. The English language changed.
   _____
5 Charles Darwin travelled to South America. He developed the theory of evolution.
   _____
6 Sailors on the *Titanic* didn't see the iceberg and 1,595 people died.
   _____

4 A ▶ 9.1 Listen and add two missing contractions to each sentence.

    'd   *would've*

1 If I ⋀ known you were coming, I ⋀ waited.
2 If I waited, I been late.
3 If I been late, I missed the show.
4 If I missed the show, I wasted my money.
5 If I wasted my money, I been angry.

B Listen again and repeat the sentences. Pay attention to the pronunciation of *had* and *would have*.

LISTENING

5 A ▶ **9.2** Look at 1–5 below and think about the question: Where and when were these things first used? Listen and complete the answers.

Invention	Where?	When?
1 toothpaste	*Egypt*	*1,600* _____ years ago
2 biological weapons	_____	_____ years ago
3 football	_____	_____ years ago
4 central heating	_____	_____ years ago
5 umbrella	_____	_____ years ago

B What is the connection between the inventions in Exercise 5A and pictures A–E below? Listen again and check.

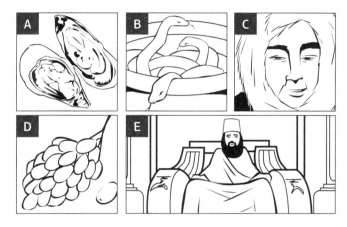

C Read these extracts from the listening in Exercise 5A and find words to match definitions a)–e) below.

1 Was it the same as modern toothpaste? Definitely not. Ancient Greek toothpaste used ingredients like crushed bones and oyster shells.

2 Some generals would even throw dead bodies at the enemy or into the enemy's river.

3 In the eighteenth century, one way American Indians were killed was through using infected blankets given to them by the Europeans who were colonising America.

4 A rich banker installed it in his house so that he could grow grapes in England's cold weather!

5 Interestingly, it seems that only kings or very important people had umbrellas in these sculptures. So they were a symbol of high social class.

a) the people that your country is fighting against in a war

_____

b) something that represents a special quality or situation

_____

c) placed somewhere and connected ready to be used

_____

d) containing dangerous bacteria which spread disease

_____

e) pressed very hard so it is broken into extremely small pieces

_____

WRITING

A SHORT ESSAY; LEARN TO STRUCTURE PARAGRAPHS

6 A Read the introduction to a short essay and choose the best title.

a) Sumerian Culture
b) The History of Writing
c) Business throughout History

In 3200 BC, Sumerians invented writing. For these people, who were located in the area we now call Iraq, there was nothing poetic about it. They didn't write to fire the imagination or to tell beautiful stories. Instead, they wrote because it was a way to keep business records. While previous generations had relied on their memory for the details of deals and the things they owned, the new generation decided to make permanent records. As a result, early 'writing' looks like a very simple type of drawing.

B Read the introduction again and:

1 Circle the topic sentence.
2 Underline a linking word (one has already been underlined).
3 Underline one linking expression (three words).

C Read the notes and finish the essay (120–150 words).

At first = pictures of animals, body parts, trees, birds, everyday tools
Then later symbols = for ideas
Then later symbols = for sounds
Could be read left to right or right to left – picture of a head (human or animal) at beginning of line showed readers the direction to read in

On walls of temples and on papyrus (early paper)
99% of people = illiterate – only religious leaders/ scholars read
Start of writing = start of 'history' – ideas and other info passed down through time

GRAMMAR

ACTIVE VERSUS PASSIVE

1 A Read the text and correct five mistakes with passives.

GENERATION Y

Millennial misery and how to get over it!

Sam is generation Y: she was been born in the 1990s and was brought up in a world of social media, technological progress and globalisation. Sam has a university education, a good standard of living and a busy social life. But she is miserable. According to recent research, unhappiness is be felt more often by this generation than the previous one.

Some of the reasons may seem obvious: for example unemployment and expensive housing are causing pressure for people. Nowadays each graduate-level job (meaning it requires university education) is chased by over 100 people and millennials are much less likely to have their own home than earlier generations. However, these are not new problems, such issues have been faced by young people for a long time. Instead some alternative reasons have be suggested by recent research: the first is that generation Y expect more from life than their parents did and are disappointed when they don't get it. While generation X hoped for a secure job, generation Y expect the job to be interesting as well as secure. Secondly, generation Y been told to believe in themselves, that they deserve success quickly. In the past, years of hard work was seen as normal while generation Y believe they should have a management level job within a few years of starting work.

It is these differences between expectation and real life that make generation Y less happy than their parents. So how can someone in the Y generation be happy? The best way is not to give up dreams but to understand that no job is perfect and any kind of success will probably only to be achieved by years of hard work.

B Read the text again and underline five correct examples of the passive.

2 A Rewrite sentences 1–6 using passives. Do not say who did the action.

1 People give the Institute a million euros a year.
   The Institute's given a million euros a year.

2 One day they will discover a cure for cancer.
   _____

3 Someone stole the files last year.
   _____

4 They took these photos at the end of the war.
   _____

5 The searchers have found the missing people.
   _____

6 Someone cleans the paintings once a year.
   _____

B ▶ **9.3** Listen and check. What happens to the pronunciation of the auxiliary verbs *are*, *were*, *has*(*n't*) *been* and *have been*? Listen again and repeat.

VOCABULARY

PERIODS OF TIME

3 Replace the underlined phrases with the phrases in the box.

> the generation   over a quarter-century   millennium
> just over a century ago   ~~era~~   half a century
> over seven decades   just over a fortnight

1 The eighteenth century was a great <u>period of time</u> for music. _____ *era* _____

2 Nelson Mandela spent <u>twenty-seven years</u> in prison.
   _____

3 <u>In 1909</u>, Geronimo, the Native American leader, died.
   _____

4 We are in the first stage of a new <u>thousand-year cycle</u>. _____

5 Louis XIV ruled France for <u>seventy-two years</u>.
   _____

6 A world full of technology is normal for <u>those people born in the 1990s</u>. _____

7 Jack Kerouac wrote *On the Road*, a classic novel about 1960s freedom, in <u>about eighteen days</u>.
   _____

8 Fidel Castro led Cuba for nearly <u>fifty years</u>.
   _____

VOCABULARY *PLUS*

COLLOCATIONS

4 A Complete phrases 1–16 with *come*, *give*, *have* or *make*. Use each verb four times.

1 _____ a good time	9 _____ directions
2 _____ progress	10 _____ trouble
3 _____ a talk	11 _____ back
4 _____ naturally	12 _____ a mess
5 _____ a break	13 _____ me a call
6 _____ a dream	14 _____ a profit
7 _____ first	15 _____ by car
8 _____ instructions	16 _____ a decision

B Complete 1–5 using two collocations with the same verb. Make sure you use the correct tense.

1 I'm _____ _____ with this report. It's really difficult to write. I think I'll _____ a _____ and finish it later.

2 In 2009 the company _____ a _____ to close its European offices. After two years, it _____ a _____ of over $1,000,000.

3 Can you _____ me a _____ when you get this message? I need you to _____ me _____ to your house. I'm completely lost!

4 Drawing didn't _____ _____ to me. It took me years to become good at it, but last year I _____ _____ in an art competition.

5 The boss is going to _____ a _____ to the employees. He wants to _____ _____ on how to use the new software.

READING

5 A Look at the table. What information do you think goes in gaps 1–6? Read the text below and check your ideas.

Name	Born	Origin of name	Known for
The Lost Generation	1 _____	Gertrude Stein, a writer, named them.	Millions died in World War I (1914–1918)
Baby Boomers	2 _____	The 'baby boom' (high birth rates) after World War II	Being successful (in USA)
Generation X	1960s and 1970s	3 _____	4 _____
Millennials (Generation Y)	5 _____	A book: *Millennials Rising: The Next Great Generation*	6 _____

Generations and Generalisations

'Young people these days! They contradict their parents, chatter in the company of guests, eat their food too quickly and are rude to their teachers!' Who said this? Was it a tired, stressed twenty-first century parent? No. These words were
5 said by Socrates in Athens two and a half thousand years ago. It seems that every generation complains about the next generation. But now there's another element: in the twentieth century we began naming each generation.

First came The Lost Generation (born around 1880–1895).
10 This was the generation which fought in World War I (1914–1918), in which over fifteen million people were killed. American writer Gertrude Stein is famous for naming it The Lost Generation, but actually it was her French car mechanic (she lived in Paris) who first used the expression. He
15 complained that the young mechanics who worked for him were useless at their jobs and he described them as *une génération perdue* – a lost generation! Stein borrowed the expression.

After the Second World War, there was the Boomer
20 Generation, or the Baby Boomers. This was the generation born between 1945 and about 1960, a period when birth rates increased throughout the world. In the USA, the Baby Boomers are seen as the great, successful generation which made their country rich.

25 The next generation was called Generation X. The name was popularised by Canadian writer Douglas Coupland in his 1991 novel, *Generation X: Tales for an Accelerated Culture*. People from Generation X – born in the 1960s and 1970s – rebelled against their parents' values. They didn't want to work for
30 the same company their whole life and they spent their time listening to 'grunge' music or playing video games.

The next generation has two names: Generation Y and the Millennials. Generation Y was first described in detail in 2000, when Neil Howe and William Strauss wrote *Millennials*
35 *Rising: The Next Great Generation*. Generation Y – people who were born in the 1980s and 1990s – is known for its love of technology: iPods, mobile phones, digital cameras, digital everything. They are amazing networkers, constantly online and great multitaskers. They can read (web pages), listen (to
40 music on their iPods) and write (Instant Messages) all at the same time.

But are these generational names correct? Can we really describe a whole generation as having similar habits and qualities? How similar are the lives of teenagers in New York
45 to the lives of teenagers in rural China or Peru? In 2010, only a quarter of the world's population used the internet. Only a small percentage of those had iPods. So can we say this generation loves technology?

Are we really talking about generations or generalisations?

B Complete the questions.

1 Q: What did _____?
  A: 'Young people these days! They contradict their parents, chatter in the company of guests, eat their food too quickly and are rude to their teachers!'
2 Q: When did we _____?
  A: In the twentieth century.
3 Q: How many _____?
  A: Over fifteen million.
4 Q: What happened _____?
  A: Birth rates increased throughout the world.
5 Q: Who _____?
  A: Neil Howe and William Strauss.
6 Q: How many _____?
  A: Twenty-five percent of the world's population.

C Match words 1–6 with definitions a)–f).

1 contradict (line 1)
2 chatter (line 2)
3 birth rate (line 22)
4 popularise (line 26)
5 networkers (line 38)
6 multitaskers (line 39)

a) make something known and liked by many people
b) people who spend a lot of time communicating and sharing information with others
c) the number of children born in a particular year/place
d) talk quickly in a friendly way about unimportant things
e) disagree, saying that the opposite is true
f) people who can do lots of things at the same time

HISTORY NOW MAGAZINE | WHO DO YOU ADMIRE?

'I admire the explorer Ranulph Fiennes. He walked to both the South and North Poles, crossed Antarctica on foot, and climbed Mount Everest when he was sixty-five. He lost fingers and toes and still kept exploring. You have to be ¹b___v__ to do that. He's very ²ch_____m_____ too: he was on a shortlist to play James Bond, but Roger Moore got the part instead! Fiennes's life has been ³ex_____y; one of his greatest achievements is that he has raised over 5 million pounds for charity.'

(Mark, climber)

'I admire Wangari Maathai. She's a Kenyan activist who founded The Green Belt Movement, an organisation that protects the environment. She has also been very ⁴i__f_____l in the women's rights movement. She was the first African woman to win the Nobel Peace Prize, which, for women all over the world, is absolutely ⁵i____p_____n____. It shows that women in poor countries can make a difference.'

(Umunyana, teacher)

'I love Ang Lee's films. I think he's the most ⁶cr_____ director working today. I've watched Crouching Tiger, Hidden Dragon seven times. I love the shots of landscapes and people flying through the air. It just seems so ⁷o_____l compared to most Hollywood films. His films are always really ⁸i_____v__ too – like Brokeback Mountain. Who could imagine a story about gay cowboys becoming a classic?'

(Hae Jin, film student)

VOCABULARY

DESCRIBING PEOPLE

1 Read the text and complete words 1–8.

FUNCTION

EXPRESSING UNCERTAINTY

2 Circle the correct option to complete the conversations.

1 A: When were the first Olympic Games?
 B: a) I have no idea.
 b) I haven't got an idea.

2 A: Do you know who invented the machine gun?
 B: a) I haven't the clue.
 b) I haven't a clue.

3 A: What's the world's biggest country?
 B: a) I'm not a hundred percent certain and it might be Russia.
 b) I'm not a hundred percent certain but it might be Russia.

4 A: Do you know when the first emails were sent?
 B: a) I'm fairly sure it was in the 1970s.
 b) I'm fair sure it was in the 1970s.

5 A: Who's the current President of South Africa?
 B: a) It's definitely but not Thabo Mbeki.
 b) It's definitely not Thabo Mbeki.

6 A: Which country has reached the World Cup final the most times?
 B: a) I don't know but I'm sure it isn't England.
 b) I don't know but I've sure it isn't England.

7 A: What year did Yuri Gagarin fly into space?
 B: a) I don't can remember.
 b) I can't remember.

8 A: What's the name of that French woman who lived to 122?
 B: a) I've forgotten.
 b) I'm forgotten.

LEARN TO

REACT TO INFORMATION

3 A Complete the conversations.

1 A: Marisa had her baby yesterday.
 B: _____ she? What wonderful news!

2 A: I'm doing an online project about Minecraft.
 B: Oh really? _____'s interesting.

3 A: His cousin was an Olympic boxer.
 B: _____ he? Wow!

4 A: My sister doesn't eat meat.
 B: _____ she? OK, I'll cook fish.

5 A: I think we need to go down this road here.
 B: That's _____! I remember that café.

6 A: I love Lady Gaga!
 B: _____ you? I think she's crazy.

7 A: Did you know that dolphins have names for each other?
 B: That's _____.

8 A: My parents have never been here.
 B: _____ they? When are they going to visit?

9 A: Jake was the number one student in the country.
 B: Really? I _____ know that.

10 A: John's got the car. We'll have to travel by bus.
 B: _____ we? Oh, that's annoying.

B ▶ **9.4** Listen and check. Then listen again and shadow B's part. Try to copy the intonation.

VOCABULARY

THE ENVIRONMENT

1 A Match the words and phrases in the box with definitions 1–10.

> processed   on standby   packaging   organic
> energy-saving   second-hand   double glazed
> recycled   pre-prepared   insulated

1 not switched off, but ready to be used when needed _____

2 windows or doors with two layers of glass _____

3 food with substances added to it in order to preserve it, improve its colour, etc. _____

4 covered with a material that stops electricity, sound, heat, etc. from getting out _____

5 grown without chemicals _____

6 food which has already been washed, prepared, cooked, etc. so that it is ready to eat _____

7 the bags, boxes, etc. that a product is sold in _____

8 using less electricity than normal _____

9 glass or paper, etc. which has been processed so that it can be used again _____

10 not new; has been owned by someone else _____

B Complete the sentences with words from Exercise 1A.

1 We don't use chemicals. All our fruit and vegetables are _____.

2 I don't buy new clothes – I buy everything from _____ shops.

3 All the windows are _____ so we can't hear the noise outside.

4 If we changed to _____ light bulbs, our electricity bills would be cheaper.

5 I don't have time to cook in the evenings, so I buy a _____ meal on the way home.

6 Everything in the café is fresh and natural. We don't use any _____ food.

7 All the paper and plastic from the office is _____ in these bins.

8 Don't leave the TV on _____. Turn it off when you go to bed.

9 I don't buy fruit in the supermarket because they use too much _____ which can't be recycled.

10 The house is much warmer now that we have _____ the roof.

LISTENING

2 A Read the text about Earth Hour. Can you complete it?

EARTH HOUR: HOW SMALL ACTION CAN HAVE A BIG IMPACT

Earth Hour is a global event where people around the world switch off the [1]_____ in their houses, offices and at other important landmarks, like the [2]_____ in Paris and the [3]_____ in Egypt. It started in 2007 in [4]_____, Australia, as a protest against climate [5]_____ and has grown into a world-wide event. But not everyone thinks it is a good idea – people have [6]_____ opinions about what an event like Earth Hour can achieve.

B ▶ 10.1 Listen to a radio phone-in programme about Earth Hour and see if you were right.

3 A Are the statements true (T) or false (F)? Correct the false statements.

1 In 2007, twenty-two million people across Sydney switched off their lights for Earth Hour.

2 In 2010, thousands of cities in 128 countries took part in the event.

3 Organisers say that they want to show what people can do to save energy.

4 Everybody agrees that the event is a good way to help people understand the problem.

5 Amy and her children had dinner by candlelight.

6 Jay-Jay thinks that the event helps people to change their everyday behaviour.

B Complete the phrases in bold so that they mean the same as the phrase in brackets.

1 One city decided to **take a** _____ **against** climate change. (protest against)

2 Earth Hour quickly **went** _____. (spread across the world)

3 In 2010, thousands of cities in 128 countries **took** _____. (participated)

4 The Eiffel Tower in Paris, the Egyptian Pyramids, New York's Empire State Building and Sydney Harbour Bridge were all _____ **into darkness**. (made to go dark quickly)

5 Organisers want to **draw** _____ **to** the problem of climate change. (make people notice)

6 Is it a good way to _____ **awareness** about the problems the world is facing? (increase the number of people who know about something)

7 I think it's a **complete** _____ **of time**. (not a good way to use time)

GRAMMAR
REPORTED SPEECH

4 Complete the reported sentences.

1 'I don't understand why you're always late.'
She said that she _____ understand why I was always late.

2 'We're meeting outside the gym at 6.15,' Bill told the others.
Bill said that they _____ meeting outside the gym at 6.15.

3 'I've eaten plenty already, thank you.'
He said that he _____ eaten plenty already.

4 'My job finished last week,' she told Jim.
She told Jim that _____ job had finished the week before.

5 'I'll see you tomorrow,' said Adam.
Adam said that he would see us the _____ day.

6 'It's my favourite programme.'
Luis told his mother that it was _____ favourite programme.

7 'We'll meet you at the airport.'
They told her that they _____ meet her at the airport.

8 'Are you enjoying the trip?' the tour leader asked.
The tour leader asked them if _____ were enjoying the trip.

5 A Ali (A) is talking to a travel agent (T) about booking a holiday. Put their conversation in the correct order.

A: _____ No, I haven't, but it's a good idea.
A: __1__ I want to go to Spain because I've never been there before.
A: _____ OK.
A: _____ I'm thinking of going by plane.
A: _____ That sounds great!
A: _____ No, I haven't. Could you show me what accommodation is available?
T: _____ Have you thought about taking the train instead?
T: _____ How are you planning to travel?
T: _____ There's an eco-farm near Valencia where you can stay for free if you help the farmer pick his olives.
T: _____ It's cheaper than flying. I'll show you some of the train routes.
T: _____ Have you decided where you want to stay?

B Complete the sentences reporting the conversation in Exercise 5A. Write one word in each gap. Contractions are one word.

1 Ali said that _she_ _wanted_ to go to Spain because _she'd_ _never_ _been_ _there_ before.
2 The travel agent _____ _____ how she _____ _____ to travel.
3 She said that _____ _____ _____ of going by plane.
4 He asked her if _____ _____ about taking the train instead.
5 Ali said that _____ _____, but that _____ _____ a good idea.
6 The travel agent said that it was cheaper than flying and that he _____ _____ _____ some of the train routes.
7 He asked her if she _____ _____ where _____ _____ to stay.
8 She said that _____ _____. She asked him to show her what accommodation was available.
9 He said that there was an eco-farm near Valencia where she _____ _____ for free if she _____ the farmer pick his olives.
10 Ali said that _____ _____.

VOCABULARY PLUS
WORD BUILDING: PREFIXES

6 Add prefixes un-, dis-, under-, mis- or re- to the words in bold to complete the sentences.

1 I _____**understood** his directions and got completely lost.
2 Discipline is very important to us. We don't like the children to _____**obey** the teacher.
3 Shall I throw these boxes away or can we _____**use** them for something else?
4 It's a very _____**usual** situation. Nothing like this has happened before.
5 I _____**estimated** how long the journey would take. It took an hour longer than I expected.
6 The old man walked around the corner and _____**appeared**. We never saw him again.
7 I don't know how you find anything in this office. It's so _____**tidy**!
8 I have to _____**new** my driving licence because it has expired.
9 They use children in their factories, which I find completely _____**ethical**.
10 I'm afraid I have to _____**agree**. I don't think that's right at all.

VOCABULARY
REPORTING VERBS

1 Circle the correct option to complete the reported statements.

1 'Can I give you a hand?'

He _____ to help.

a) invited   **b)** refused   **c)** offered

2 'I'm afraid the first train leaves at 6.30a.m.'

She _____ that the first train leaves at 6.30a.m.

a) offered   **b)** explained   **c)** suggested

3 'I don't believe you!'

He _____ to believe me.

a) refused   **b)** promised   **c)** offered

4 'Come in and have something to eat.'

She _____ us in for something to eat.

a) offered   **b)** warned   **c)** invited

5 'Don't go there. It's dangerous.'

He _____ us not to go there.

a) warned   **b)** suggested **c)** invited

6 'I'll buy you a diamond ring.'

He _____ to buy me a diamond ring.

a) explained **b)** promised   **c)** suggested

7 'Why don't we go for a walk?'

He _____ going for a walk.

a) warned   **b)** offered   **c)** suggested

READING

2 Read the article and match pictures A–E with paragraphs 1–5.

A

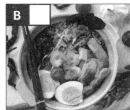
B

C

D

E

A TASTE OF YOUR LIFE

1 In the BBC chat show series *A Taste of My Life*, TV chef Nigel Slater talks to celebrities about their strongest food memories and particular dishes which have shaped their lives. Comic actor Sanjeev Bhaskar reminisces about the contrast between bland 'meat and two veg' school dinners and the Indian food he was served at home. Fellow chef Nigella Lawson tells her life story through food. Do you have a memory of a favourite dish associated with a special event? Can you remember who cooked it? We asked for your best food memories.

2 It has to be **boiled** eggs with 'soldiers'. My mum used to give this to us as kids. The egg should be soft-boiled so the **yolk** is still **runny**, and the toast is spread with melted butter and cut into thin strips (tall and straight, like soldiers), which you can hold and dip into the top of the egg. Now I give it to my kids and they love it. It's healthy and I hope it will give them the same happy memories.
Claire, UK

3 My grandmother's homemade pasta. She used to make pasta on the kitchen table every day. I can remember her laying out the pasta in the morning when I got up for breakfast. Nowadays, people have pasta machines, but she would roll out the pasta by hand, and when we came home from school, there was always a plate of fresh **tagliatelle** waiting for us. The dry pasta you buy in the shops just doesn't taste the same.
Mariella, Italy

4 Tortilla. Whenever I feel like I'm missing my home country, I cook a tortilla. It's a kind of omelette made with potato and onion and you can find it in all the tapas bars in Spain. But, of course, the one I make at home is the best. I have so many happy memories of eating tortilla. They go all through my life, from when I was a child, a student at university, eating with friends. Tortilla is everywhere. I couldn't live without it.
Jorge, Spain

5 When I go back to Penang (Malaysia), I go straight to a hawker (street seller) and order a bowl of Penang Hokkien Mee (prawn noodle soup). It's one dish I always **miss**. There is something about the combination of the prawns and the chilli in the soup with the noodles. I just love it. You can make it at home too, but it tastes better when you eat it out on the street. There's an atmosphere, with the heat, and the noise of the traffic and people shouting. It's more than just a dish — it's an experience. And I always look forward to it. Penang's food is part of my life. In fact, I don't think you can find the same taste anywhere else.
Irene, US

3 Read the article again and answer the questions.

1 Who has happy memories of the dish from different stages of their life? _____

2 Who likes to eat this dish when they return to a special place? _____

3 Who feeds her children a dish which her mother fed her as a child? _____

4 Who describes how the dish should be prepared? _____

5 Who remembers eating this dish when they came home from school as a child? _____

6 Who thinks the dish tastes better when you eat in on the street? _____

4 Underline the correct alternative for these words and phrases from the article.

1 reminisces: talk or think about *pleasant/terrible* events in your past

2 boiled: cooked in *oil/water*

3 yolk: the *yellow middle/shell* of an egg

4 runny: *hard/soft; liquid*

5 tagliatelle: a type of *pasta/soup*

6 miss: feel *sad because you haven't got/happy because you have got* something you like

GRAMMAR
VERB PATTERNS

5 Complete the email with verb patterns which include the verbs in brackets. You may need to add personal pronouns (e.g. *us, me*).

> Hi Francesca,
>
> How are things? We've just had a great weekend. Ali and Greg are over from New Zealand, so we ¹ _decided to meet_ (decide/meet) up. They wanted to see London, so I ² _____ (suggest/spend) a couple of days there. Louise ³ _____ (invite/stay) at her place, which made things easier. She also ⁴ _____ (offer/take) some time off work, so she could show us around the sights. She ⁵ _____ (explain/be) easier to travel around with someone who knows where everything is. We were planning to get an organised bus tour, but Louise ⁶ _____ (recommend/travel) by ourselves on the buses and Underground. It was a great way to see the city. There were so many things we all wanted to see, but we ⁷ _____ (agree/choose) one or two things each. I was really keen to go on the London Eye, but Louise ⁸ _____ (warn/not go) up because the weather was bad. We saw lots of other things though, like Big Ben and the Tate Modern. I ⁹ _____ (promise/write) and tell you all about it. Next time, you must come, too!
>
> Hope you're well. Take care.
>
> Matt

6 A Complete the second sentence so that it has the same meaning as the first. Use the correct form of the words in capitals. Use between two and five words.

1 'I'm not coming with you,' said Gina. REFUSE
   Gina _____ with us.
2 'I'll definitely call you later,' he said. PROMISE
   He _____ me later.
3 'Let's go out for a meal,' they said. DECIDE
   They _____ out for a meal.
4 'OK. We won't go on holiday this year,' they said. AGREE
   They _____ on holiday this year.
5 'It's a very expensive restaurant,' she told us. WARN
   She _____ the restaurant was very expensive.
6 'James, why don't you come to the theatre with us on Friday?' they asked. INVITE
   They _____ to the theatre with them on Friday.
7 'The children grow vegetables in the garden.' EXPLAIN
   The teacher _____ grow vegetables in the garden.
8 'You should buy your fruit at the market.' RECOMMEND
   He _____ our fruit at the market.

B ▶ **10.2** Listen and check. Then listen and repeat. What happens to the words *to, for, at* and *that* in the sentences? Are they stressed or unstressed?

WRITING
A RESTAURANT REVIEW; LEARN TO LINK IDEAS

7 A Read the review. Does the writer recommend the restaurant? Why/Why not?

> ## *Tiffany's*
>
> A colleague of mine recommended Tiffany's.
>
> Perhaps I should just say that I won't be following his recommendations any more. As I walked in, the first things I noticed were the large flat-screen TVs all over the restaurant, each one showing a different football game. ¹_____. My first reaction was to walk straight out, but there were quite a lot of people there and we were hungry, so we decided to stay and see what the food was like.
>
> First of all, we ordered drinks. When they arrived, the waitress had forgotten the water, none of the drinks had ice and ²_____. We didn't see the waitress again for about another twenty minutes. When she finally reappeared, we tried to order some food. I was amazed when she didn't even write down our order. ³_____. I'm sorry, but a good waiter or waitress will always write down what you want.
>
> The starters arrived, but they were very small. ⁴_____. I ate it, but it was nothing special. If you're looking for somewhere nice to eat then I wouldn't choose Tiffany's, ⁵_____.

B Complete phrases a)–e) with the words in the box. Then match them with gaps 1–5 in the review.

> unless   such   so   while   although   that

a) one of the glasses was _____ dirty that we sent it back
b) _____ the main courses were a little better, my fish was fried and not grilled as I had asked for
c) _____ you just want to enjoy the football
d) She thought she had _____ a good memory _____ she would remember everything
e) _____ the décor was bright and fun-looking, the atmosphere was uninviting and the chairs weren't comfortable at all

8 A Read the review again and tick the information it gives. Which information is not given?

1 information about the price
2 information about the menu and type of food served
3 details of the restaurant (name, location, phone number, etc.)
4 information about the service
5 information about the atmosphere

B Write a review of a restaurant that someone has recommended to you (180–220 words). Try to include all the information in Exercise 8A.

VOCABULARY

AIRPORTS

1 Add vowels to complete the words in the texts.

'I was travelling from Italy to Stockholm for work. In a hurry, I picked up my ¹p__ssp__rt and ticket and left for the airport without checking them. When I went to ²ch__ck __n my bags, instead of asking me if I wanted an ³__ __sl__ or a window seat and giving me my ⁴b__ __rd__ng c__rd, the lady behind the desk told me I was at the wrong airport! How was I to know that there were two airports in Milan? I was in the wrong one.'

'I couldn't believe what was happening when I tried to fly to Houston with my son last month. We had just been through the ⁵X-r__y m__ch__n__ when we were stopped by security guards and told we were not allowed to ⁶b__ __rd the plane.

The reason? My son's name, Matthew Gardner, was on a list of wanted criminals. The unbelievable thing is that my son is two years old. Apparently he was 'wanted' in connection with a shooting!'

'While waiting for a connecting flight at Hong Kong airport, I decided to do some shopping. I had a ⁷pr__ __ r__ty b__ __rd__ng card, but I forgot to keep my eye on the departure boards. One minute before my flight was due to leave, I realised to my horror that the message on the departure board read 'Flight XYZ to London – Please ⁸pr__c__ __d t__ g__t__ n__mb__r 143. Final call.' I grabbed my ⁹h__nd l__gg__g__ and ran to the gate like a marathon runner. When I boarded the plane, everyone was staring at me. As if that wasn't bad enough, when I finally found my seat, I realised I'd left my shopping bag, with my new $250 camera in it, in the duty-free shop!'

FUNCTION

GIVING ADVICE/WARNINGS

2 Circle the correct option to complete the advice/warnings.

1 Watch _____ for crocodiles. The river is full of them.
   a) up   **b)** out   **c)** at

2 Don't walk around outside without a sunhat _____ sunstroke.
   a) or to get
   b) or you will getting
   c) or else you'll get

3 Make _____ plenty of water with you. You'll be thirsty by the time you get to the top.
   a) sure you take
   b) sure of taking
   c) be sure to

4 _____ leave your bags here and we'll bring them up for you.
   a) You will better   **b)** You'd better
   c) You're better

5 If I were you, _____ the airport to see if the flight has been delayed.
   a) I'm calling   **b)** I'll call   **c)** I'd call

6 _____ book a taxi to pick you up from the airport.
   a) Don't forget   **b)** Don't forget to
   c) Do you forget

7 _____, don't forget your phrasebook. You'll need it if you can't speak the language.
   a) Whatever you do
   b) What you do
   c) Ever what you do

LEARN TO

MAKE GENERALISATIONS

3 Match 1–6 with a)–f) to make generalisations.

1 Italians have a tendency
2 Generally, people eat
3 English people often
4 In Turkey, it's common to find
5 On the whole, grandparents in China
6 In Latin cultures, the family tends to

a) later in Spain.
b) be very important.
c) to drink coffee, not tea.
d) different styles of cooking in different parts of the country.
e) are very involved in bringing up their grandchildren.
f) complain about the weather.

VOCABULARY HISTORY

1 Complete the words in these sentences.

1 The government was removed during the rev_____.

2 The change to farming communities was history's greatest tur_____ p_____.

3 Rich countries should help poor countries in their economic dev_____.

4 Because people lived close together, the disease quickly spr_____.

5 In the fight to cure cancer, the result of this research is a great adv_____.

6 She was one of the most important people in the women's mov_____.

7 The personal computer was the twentieth century's best inv_____.

8 The invention of the wheel provided the fou_____ for most machines.

9 The 3,000-year-old body found in the mountains was a great dis_____.

10 In the debate about climate change, we haven't made much pro_____.

GRAMMAR HYPOTHETICAL CONDITIONAL: PAST

2 Complete the sentences with the correct form of the verbs in brackets.

1 If Xiulin _____ (not help) us, we _____ (not finish) the project on time.

2 They _____ (go) for a picnic if it _____ (not rain).

3 If I _____ (study), I _____ (not fail) the test.

4 My wife _____ (tell) me if she _____ (have) a problem.

5 If Thierry _____ (not score) that goal, we _____ (not won).

6 What _____ (you/do) if you _____ (miss) the plane?

GRAMMAR ACTIVE VERSUS PASSIVE

3 Rewrite the sentences using the passive.

1 We sell chairs and tables here.
Chairs and tables _____.

2 They don't produce coffee in England.
Coffee _____.

3 They are building a new school.
A new school _____.

4 Someone assassinated the President.
The President _____.

5 Samuel Beckett didn't write *Ulysses*.
Ulysses _____.

6 No one has told us anything about the exam.
We _____.

VOCABULARY PERIODS OF TIME

4 Underline the correct alternative.

1 There was a big party to celebrate the new *millennium/fortnight/seventies*.

2 I stayed for *the eighties/a generation/a decade*, arriving in 1989 and leaving in 1999.

3 In the first part of July, we spent *an era/a fortnight/the century* in Greece, on holiday.

4 She worked in the same school for nearly *an age/the nineties/a quarter-century*.

5 War was a way of life for my grandfather's *generation/decade/age*.

6 I grew up in *a century/an era/the nineties*.

VOCABULARY PLUS COLLOCATIONS WITH *COME, GIVE, HAVE AND MAKE*

5 Cross out the word which is **not** possible.

1 The team came *first/by car/well*.

2 I listened while Sam gave *directions/a discussion/instructions*.

3 William made *project/progress/a mess* in his art class.

4 I had a *dream/homework/good time* last night.

5 My ability to speak French came *naturally/forward/back* to me.

6 She's going to give *a talk/me a call/problem* today.

7 The company has to make a *profit/money/decision*.

8 She sometimes has *progress/trouble/a break* while doing her homework.

VOCABULARY DESCRIBING PEOPLE

6 Put the letters in bold in the correct order to complete the sentences.

1 I like **tearceiv** _____ people who have their own ideas.

2 She wasn't very **igolirna** _____; her ideas were nothing new.

3 Like most great leaders, he's very **arccisahtmi** _____.

4 Her life, spent helping others, was **xaeeyplrm** _____.

5 She had some **nnvvatiioe** _____ ideas about design.

6 Like many soldiers, he was extremely **reabv** _____.

7 My boss is **spiirotilnnaa** _____ – everyone follows him.

8 Jackson is the most **neflliunati** _____ player in the team.

FUNCTION EXPRESSING UNCERTAINTY

7 Make sentences with a word or phrase from each section.

1 I've	a) sure	i) clue.
2 I haven't	b) forgotten	ii) isn't Elizabeth.
3 I'm fairly	c) a	iii) it's Jane.
4 It's	d) it	iv) not Sarah.
5 I'm sure	e) no	v) her name.
6 I have	f) definitely	vi) idea.

1 *I've forgotten her name.*
2 ________
3 ________
4 ________
5 ________
6 ________

LEARN TO REACT TO INFORMATION

8 Underline the correct alternative.

1 **A:** This film is very similar to his last one.
B: I was *about just/just about* to say that.
2 **A:** Jeanette Winterson is the one who wrote *The Passion*.
B: *Does/Is* she? I didn't know that.
3 **A:** It took over a hundred years to complete the building.
B: Did it? That's *interesting/too interesting*.
4 **A:** *Whole Lotta Love* was written by Led Zeppelin.
B: I knew that. I just *don't/couldn't* remember.

VOCABULARY THE ENVIRONMENT

9 Complete the sentences with the words in the box.

packaging	double glazed	recycled	energy-saving
pre-prepared	on standby	~~processed~~	insulated
organic	second-hand		

1 We try not to eat too much *processed* food and we grow our own ________ vegetables.
2 We are very conscious of the environment: we use ________ light bulbs and the house is ________.
3 We don't waste energy. Our windows are ________ and we make sure our computers are ________ or switched off.
4 We rarely buy ________ food. The ________ is such a waste of plastic.
5 All of our clothes are ________ and most of our furniture is ________.

GRAMMAR REPORTED SPEECH

10 Complete the conversations. B always remembers that A said the opposite earlier.

1 **A:** That book is very good.
B: Oh? I thought you said *that book wasn't very good*.
2 **A:** I know the answer.
B: Oh? I thought you said ________.
3 **A:** I haven't been to Germany.
B: Oh? I thought you said ________.
4 **A:** I can't swim.
B: Oh? I thought you said ________.
5 **A:** I'm going to university.
B: Oh? I thought you said ________.
6 **A:** I won't be there on Monday.
B: Oh? I thought you said ________.
7 **A:** I'll be able to help.
B: Oh? I thought you said ________.
8 **A:** I spoke to Kevin.
B: Oh? I thought you said ________.

11 Find and correct five mistakes in the reported questions below.

1 He asked me when started the game.
2 He asked me if I do play any instruments.
3 She asked me where my husband was.
4 She asked me if I worked at home.
5 He asked me why was I crying.
6 She asked me if slept my baby all night.
7 She asked me if they did speak English.

VOCABULARY PLUS WORD BUILDING: PREFIXES

12 Add prefixes to two words in each sentence.

1 Ah, I *mis*understood the instructions; I thought it was *un*usual to cook pasta for forty minutes!
2 He judged the cooking time and left the food in the oven too long; now it's cooked.
3 The results of his diet are believable; he used to be weight but now he looks fit.
4 The kitchen was tidy so I told her to put things in order but she obeyed me and went out.
5 We use plastic plates instead of throwing them away and we cycle food packaging.
6 I approved of Dr Kim's behaviour because it's ethical to give bad advice to patients.
7 Don't estimate the time it takes to new a passport; mine took over two months.
8 He was living here, then he suddenly appeared; at the moment his location is known.

VOCABULARY REPORTING VERBS

13 Underline one incorrect verb in each sentence. Which sentence does it belong to?

1 David promised us to his birthday party. *Sentence 6*
2 The tour guide refused us about poisonous spiders.
3 The doorman suggested to let me into the club because I was wearing jeans.
4 I explained to take her for dinner to say 'thank you'.
5 The teacher invited the grammar clearly so everyone understood.
6 My dad warned to buy me an ice cream if I behaved well.
7 Minty offered going to Greece for our holiday.

GRAMMAR VERB PATTERNS

14 Underline the correct alternatives.

WORLD FOOD
RESTAURANT

A friend suggested ¹*for me/that I/me to* go to World Food and explained ²*me/that/if* I would love the cool, relaxed atmosphere and the outstanding menu. He warned ³*me to/that I/ me* expect a big bill at the end but promised ⁴*me/to/which* that it was worth it.

I arrived at 7.25 for a 7.30 reservation and the receptionist told me ⁵*waiting/wait/to wait* in the bar. I waited for thirty-five minutes before a waiter, with no apology, offered ⁶*for take/ taking/to take* me to my table.

The decor was horrible – grey paintings that looked like something your dog might bring home – and I was seated under a speaker playing loud music. I asked the waiter ⁷*give/for give/to give* me a better seat. At first he refused ⁸*to move/moving/move* me, saying the restaurant was full, but finally he agreed ⁹*for/that he/to* give me a window seat.

After the terrible service, I feared the worst, but the food was excellent. My friend had recommended ¹⁰*to try/by trying/trying* the salmon in teriyaki sauce. It was a great choice, as was the apple pie I had for dessert. All World Food needs is a new attitude; the cooking is outstanding.

VOCABULARY AIRPORTS

15 Match 1–8 with a)–h) to make sentences you hear at an airport.

1 May I see
2 Please proceed
3 Is this hand
4 Would you like to check
5 15D is an aisle
6 Your flight will
7 Can I see your boarding
8 We don't have a gate

a) to gate number 62.
b) seat, sir.
c) card, please?
d) your passport, please?
e) luggage, madam?
f) number yet.
g) in this bag?
h) board at 2.45.

FUNCTION GIVING ADVICE/WARNINGS; MAKING GENERALISATIONS

16 Put the words in italics in the correct order to complete the sentences.

Q I'm exploring the Amazon for a few weeks. Can you give me some advice?

A OK, ¹*thing is the important to most* _____ be prepared. Read about the Amazon first. Regarding clothes, ²*sure bring you make* _____ a raincoat as it's very wet. Obviously, it's really wild so ³*snakes watch for out* _____. The truth is ⁴*common not very it's* _____ for people to die from snakebites in the Amazon, but it does happen.

Q I'm climbing Mount Kilimanjaro. Any tips?

A Kilimanjaro is a tough climb, so ⁵*I you, if start I'd were* _____ preparing physically four months before the trip. Also, ⁶*bring to need you* _____ a really good pair of hiking boots. Finally, climbers ⁷*bring tendency a to have* _____ too much stuff. ⁸*you pack don't do, Whatever* _____ too much. You'll have to carry it all up the mountain.

Q I'm travelling around India. Can you give me some advice?

A Firstly, you'll see some amazing sights, so ⁹*bring forget don't to* _____ a camera. Secondly, ¹⁰*whole the on* _____ Indian food is wonderful, but ¹¹*eat careful be to* _____ only food that has been prepared properly in a kitchen. Also, ¹²*some take better you'd* _____ water-purifying pills because the water can be contaminated.

CHECK

Circle the correct option to complete the sentences.

1 The _____ of penicillin was an accident.
   a) discovery   **b)** discoverer   **c)** discover

2 Because of the internet, ideas _____ quickly.
   a) revolution   **b)** invent   **c)** spread

3 He wouldn't have survived if he _____ his medicine.
   a) took   **b)** hadn't taken   **c)** hasn't taken

4 If you had seen her, what _____?
   a) did you say   **b)** would you said   **c)** would you have said

5 If I _____ that it was so hard, I would have asked for help.
   a) would have known   **b)** knew   **c)** 'd known

6 She would _____ famous if she'd been born in another generation.
   a) have be   **b)** have been   **c)** had been

7 All articles _____ by our board of editors.
   a) are discussed   **b)** discussed   **c)** be discussed

8 Why _____ about this problem?
   a) wasn't I told   **b)** was I told not   **c)** I wasn't told

9 The money will _____ tomorrow.
   a) collect   **b)** to be collected   **c)** be collected

10 The 1980s was my favourite _____.
   a) century   **b)** millennium   **c)** decade

11 We are making _____ all the time.
   a) movement   **b)** progress   **c)** advance

12 Lu _____ us directions to her house.
   a) did   **b)** gave   **c)** had

13 She was a very _____ musician.
   a) influencing   **b)** inspiration   **c)** influential

14 I have _____ what to do.
   a) a clue   **b)** no idea   **c)** ideas

15 I'm a hundred percent _____ of the answer.
   a) knowing   **b)** certainly   **c)** certain

16 We never eat _____ food.
   a) processed   **b)** process   **c)** reused

17 She said she _____ to talk to her boss.
   a) was going   **b)** going   **c)** would

18 You told me you _____ Bill for years.
   a) haven't to see   **b)** don't see   **c)** hadn't seen

19 He asked me when _____ in the country.
   a) I arrive   **b)** I'd arrived   **c)** I'm arrive

20 She asked if we _____ how to get to Bristol.
   a) are knowing   **b)** did know   **c)** knew

21 I _____ the question.
   a) disunderstood   **b)** not understand
   c) misunderstood

22 I _____ to pay the bill but she refused.
   a) offered   **b)** explained   **c)** invited

23 She _____ them that the water was dangerous.
   a) refused   **b)** warned   **c)** suggested

24 The man refused _____ me the gun.
   a) giving   **b)** for give   **c)** to give

25 The guide recommended _____ the museum.
   a) visiting   **b)** to visit   **c)** visit

26 My mother suggests _____ early as it gets crowded.
   a) that we are go   **b)** that we go   **c)** us to go

27 I warned you _____ that.
   a) not doing   **b)** not to do   **c)** to not do

28 I took it on the plane as hand _____.
   a) luggage   **b)** cases   **c)** bags

29 If I _____ pack some spare shoes.
   a) were you, you should   **b)** were you, I'd
   c) 'm you, I'd

30 Please make _____ you sign your name.
   a) definite   **b)** sure   **c)** certainly

RESULT   /30

73

AUDIO SCRIPTS

UNIT 1 Recording 1

1 When's the best time to learn a language?
2 Who taught you English first?
3 Where's the dictionary?
4 Why did people stop speaking Latin every day?
5 What did you learn last lesson?
6 What does your name mean?

UNIT 1 Recording 2

Maria

My mum and dad didn't speak any other languages at home, only German. But when I started school they were really keen for me to learn English – my mother said it would give me a lot of job opportunities. Luckily, I think I had a natural talent and it's something I was interested in anyway so I enjoyed my lessons. I think my mum encouraged me because she liked travelling so much. We used to visit different countries every year, mostly in Europe, but one year we went to Thailand and I absolutely loved it. Everything was so different. It was a culture shock but in a good way! That's probably why I became a translator, actually, because of my mum encouraging me to learn other languages and visit other countries. I'm pleased she did. I feel very lucky that I meet people from all around the world.

Ahmed

Well, Lebanon is a beautiful country and living in Beirut always felt very cosmopolitan. I mean when you walk down the street you hear Arabic, French, English – all sorts. A lot of the population there speak more than one language. I like that. It's a great experience, I think. You understand that the world is full of different people and different cultures. And it's pretty similar in the Netherlands too, I guess. When I moved there to work I couldn't speak Dutch or Flemish. I mostly communicated in English to start with. To be honest, it didn't actually cause many problems because people there are usually fluent in English. But I did some part-time Dutch lessons at college in the evenings and by the end of the first year I could get by. I hope I'm pretty fluent nowadays but you'd have to ask my Dutch friends!

Jessie

I think in the UK we aren't brilliant at learning new languages. I think people would like to learn but because English is so common everywhere people don't always feel a pressure to speak other languages. And when Brits travel they can generally use English, which is a shame because practice is so important with that kind of thing. I only learnt Japanese because I was living in Japan for a while. I worked for an international company and spent a couple of years in Tokyo. I didn't have lessons. I picked it up in my day-to-day life. To begin with I could only use the basics – *hello, how are you*, that kind of thing. But I gradually built up my knowledge. I wasn't fluent when I left but I had basic communication skills and I could do most day-to-day things – shopping, arranging to meet people, everyday stuff.

UNIT 1 Recording 3

1 He was an employee here.
2 I had a wonderful mentor.
3 All pupils wear a uniform.
4 We were team-mates for years.
5 Have you met my fiancée?
6 Talk to your partner.
7 She's my godmother.
8 That club is for members only.

UNIT 2 Recording 1

1 A: Have you been here before?
   B: Yes, we've visited Naples a few times.
2 A: Have you had time to see the museum yet?
   B: No, we haven't had time.
3 A: Did you find your hotel OK?
   B: Yes, we found the hotel without any problems.
4 A: Have you got your guidebook?
   B: Oh no. I've left it in my room.
5 A: Have you had any lunch?
   B: Yes, we've already eaten.
6 A: Have you enjoyed your stay?
   B: Yes, we've had a wonderful time.

UNIT 2 Recording 2

1 Christine

A lot of friends were staying in my apartment. We'd had a party the night before, and in the morning, one friend, Danny, got up to make everyone some coffee. While he was making the coffee, he heard the news on the radio. He came back into the room and told us that John Lennon had died. Someone had shot John Lennon. We were all really shocked. It was a very strange feeling. We couldn't believe it. We had all grown up with the music of John Lennon and The Beatles. We had played his music the night before. And now, suddenly, he was dead. There was a huge feeling of loss. He was such a peaceful man, who had wanted peace for everyone. It was a terrible way for him to die.

2 Rob

I was travelling to a meeting on the Tube that morning and there were delays everywhere. They closed the Underground station. At first, I was really angry, and worried about not getting to my meeting on time. But gradually, we started to realise that something terrible had happened. People outside the station were trying to talk on their mobile phones but the networks were all down because of the panic. Some people started to get news and soon we discovered there had been bombs all over London. It was a strange and terrible feeling. There were crowds of people outside shops, watching the news on the televisions.

3 Gino

I was sitting in the kitchen of my house in Italy with my family and I was only a child. Everyone was watching television. I remember the black and white pictures. I watched as this man landed on the Moon. And I can remember thinking how amazing it must be to be an astronaut and what an exciting job it was. Until then, I had wanted to be a train driver, but for a few years afterwards, I definitely wanted to be an astronaut.

4 Marianne

I was staying in Los Angeles with some friends and I was only about eighteen years old. In the night I suddenly woke up and the whole house was shaking. I had never felt an earthquake before, but I knew that was what was happening. It was very frightening. But after a few seconds it stopped, everything went quiet and I went back to sleep. When I woke up in the morning, I thought perhaps it had all been a dream. But when I went downstairs and turned on the radio, I heard the news. The quake was in San Francisco and it had done a lot of damage. So, I was lucky really. But I will never forget that feeling.

R1 Recording 1

1 Who do you work for?
2 What type of things do you do?
3 What problems do you deal with?
4 When did you start working there?
5 Do you enjoy the job?
6 So why did you apply for this job?

R1 Recording 2

1 I've stopped.
2 We made it.
3 He helped me.
4 They've killed it.
5 You've worked hard.
6 I thanked her.

UNIT 3 Recording 1

Ruth

I'm going to backpack around Poland next month with my friend so I've already started making plans. I'm afraid I have to organise things in massive detail or I get worried. I do everything ahead of time. My friend says I plan too much but that's just me. We're travelling by ferry and bus and then doing a lot of walking so it'll be reasonably cheap. We might stay in hotels if we can find some cheap ones but we'll probably try and find youth hostels most of the time. I've booked our travel tickets and now I'm making a list of the best hostels in the cities we're visiting. Actually I really want to visit Lodz – it's the third biggest city in Poland and there's a lot of unusual street art there on the walls of buildings. I'm a graphic designer so I'm really interested in art. And these pictures are huge – on the sides of buildings – so you see them as you wander around the city. I'm organising a route around the streets so I see the best artwork. I think it's going to be fantastic. I'm going to take loads of photos, too.

Kieron

I'd like to think I'm well organised, meet deadlines and so on. For example, I'm going to a sports tournament next week – I've been playing rugby for a long time and this year we've made it to the final matches. So I've got started and written a list of things to pack, the sports kit I need and where to meet the team bus and so on. But the truth is I'm good on paper and then I procrastinate in real life. So I know that I'll put off packing until the last minute despite my plans. I'm going to try and organise myself earlier but if I'm honest I'll probably end up doing it about an hour before I leave, even though the list has been ready for a week. And I'll probably get distracted and forget something really important like my rugby boots.

Amber

I've recently started work as a party planner. We arrange unusual or specialist events, the kind of thing people can't do easily themselves. In my own life I don't plan that much to be honest, I prefer to just let things happen without worrying too much. But at work I'm pretty good at organising things and multitasking. My first big event is happening next week. It's an eighteenth birthday party for a boy who really likes scuba diving. So his parents asked us to organise his party at the beach and arrange for all the guests to dive. I even went and tried it out myself! I think it'll be quite an interesting party. We'll have a diving teacher to help people who want to try it, drinks and then a barbecue and cake and so on. I hope it'll be successful, especially as it's my first party. I think planning comes naturally to me and I love meeting new people so this job suits me perfectly. Even when I was a child I used to love organising things for other people – I used to drive my mum mad because I was so bossy. But I try to keep it balanced. I don't plan much at all for myself. I just see what happens and go with that!

UNIT 3 Recording 2

1 They're <u>going</u> to <u>play squash</u>.
2 I'm going to <u>buy</u> a new <u>phone</u>.
3 She's going to spend a <u>week</u> in <u>Greece</u>.
4 He <u>isn't</u> going to <u>eat</u> anything.
5 Are you <u>going</u> to <u>walk</u> to the <u>station</u>?
6 He's going to <u>change</u> his <u>job</u>.

UNIT 3 Recording 3

Conversation 1

A: Hello? I'm trying to find my lost luggage.
B: Ah, OK.
A: My bags went missing in Montevideo in Uruguay, after a flight from Curitiba, Brazil.
B: Can you say that again? Montevideo?
A: I flew from Curitiba to Montevideo and my bags went missing.
B: Have you reported it already?
A: Yes, the name is Anders Kleeburg.
B: Hang on. Could you repeat the last name? Anders …?
A: Kleeburg. K-l-e-e-b-u-r-g.

Conversation 2

A: OK, so cricket. So this is the bowler, OK? He runs up and bowls at the batsman.
B: What exactly do you mean? What's a bowler?
A: A bowler is the person with the ball in his hand, OK? And he tries to get the batsman out. Get him off the field.
B: Do you mean to say he tries to kill the batsman with the ball?
A: No!

Conversation 3

A: Did you read this?! About popcorn. In 1948, two American scientists found some popcorn in a cave in New Mexico and dated it. It was over five thousand years old.
B: I didn't catch any of that. Are you talking about popcorn?
A: Yeah, it's an ancient food. Popcorn is thousands of years old.
B: I don't get what you're saying. You mean the popcorn we ate in the cinema yesterday is thousands of years old!
A: No! Popcorn in general. People have eaten it for thousands of years.

UNIT 4 Recording 1

1 I work in a busy airport in France. I am responsible for a small group of people. In my job you need to know what you are doing. You must be very accurate and observant. And you have to be able to work well under pressure and be a good decision maker.

2 I work in a pizza restaurant. In my job you need to have a friendly, relaxed manner. It's important to be friendly to customers, and patient. You have to be organised and have a good memory, too.

3 In my job you have to be a really good communicator. You need to be able to listen carefully to customers and find out what the problem is. And then you have to be able to think outside the box sometimes to see if you can find a solution to the problem which will keep everybody happy. You have to be able to stay calm, even if the customer starts getting angry.

4 I work in a lawyer's office. You have to have good organisational skills, I think, and you shouldn't get stressed too easily. You have to be quite hard-working as well. And you need to pay attention to detail.

5 I work in a children's hospital. I think the most important quality for my job is that you must be a caring person. You have to care about the people you're looking after. And you have to get on with children. That's very important.

6 You need to be very patient in my job, especially when there's a lot of traffic. And you have to be a good timekeeper as well. You always have to be on time.

UNIT 4 Recording 2

1 I used to be very sporty.
2 Can I use your phone?
3 He never used to worry about it.
4 I used to live in the USA when I was 18.
5 This stuff is used to kill insects.
6 I don't use the car much any more.
7 We used to love going there on holiday.
8 I didn't use to live in Europe.

R 2 Recording 1

amazing
successful
delicious
exhausted
salary
interview
furious
difficult
tasty
leader
boiling
freezing
competitive
impossible

UNIT 5 Recording 1

Mia

Well, it's changed a lot, goodness, enormously. I mean thirty years ago, I was still at school. I was ten years old. Life was a lot simpler then. All I had to think about was doing my homework and enjoying my free time with friends. I think life was simpler for everybody then. We didn't have all this technology and I think the pace of life was slower. At work, when someone sent a letter, it could take a week or two even before they would get a reply. Nowadays, people email and they expect an instant response. On the same day or within an hour or two. That puts a lot of pressure on people. We say that technology has saved us time, but it just speeds things up, and we're expected to do so much more. It's non-stop. We have mobile phones and BlackBerries, iPhones. So we don't just turn off and relax.

Tom

That's an interesting question. It's changed a lot. I live in Beijing. So there has been a huge advancement of technology and huge growth. There are more people, with more money. There has been an economic explosion here, so the city has grown. All the offices and high-rise buildings, lots of those weren't here thirty years ago. And it's very multicultural nowadays. People from all over the world live in Beijing. People came from everywhere to see if they could get rich, and many of them did get rich. They made millions. I think in a lot of places out in the countryside, things haven't changed that much. Life is quite similar to how it was before for farmers and their families. I suppose they have more technology now. They have mobile phones, and televisions, and the internet, so they know a lot more about the wider world and what is going on. Thirty years ago, they just had a radio and it was difficult to find out information. That's much easier now.

Owen

Oh, well, both probably. The world is getting better in many ways. I think if we look at living standards across the world, obviously there are still millions of people living in terrible poverty, but I think the situation is getting better. People have better access to food and medicines and education. So, these are all things which are improving. Medicine is improving, so people live longer and we can fight infectious diseases. People's lives have improved because of technology, so life is easier now than it was before. A lot of manual work is done by machines. But in some ways, the world is getting worse. War, for example, is a bigger problem all the time. There are more and more wars, which is surprising. And weapons are becoming even more dangerous. I think the environment is definitely suffering, so we are polluting more than we used to because of all the industrialisation. And I think also, socially, things are getting worse. Because people are less social now than before. They spend more time on their own, with computers and computer games, and less time talking to others, working together, and I think that is a great shame and a problem for the future, too.

UNIT 5 Recording 2

/eɪ/ make
space
communications
aeroplanes
vaccinations
/æ/ apple
antibiotics
travel
satellites
vacuum
/ə/ polar
nuclear
machine
commercial
solar

UNIT 5 Recording 3

1 A: Have you met Yinka's parents?
   B: Only once. They're doctors, aren't they?
2 A: There isn't a cloud in the sky.
   B: I know. It's a beautiful day, isn't it?
3 A: Are you looking for the scissors?
   B: You haven't seen them, have you?
4 A: Have you read Jhumpa Lahiri's new book?
   B: Yeah, she's a great writer, isn't she?
5 A: I've got my final exam tomorrow.
   B: You'll pass, won't you?
6 A: I think this is the wrong address.
   B: Yes, we've made a mistake, haven't we?

UNIT 5 Recording 4

1 A: Excuse me, could you tell me the way to the swimming pool, please?
  B: Yes, of course I can. You keep going this way, until you get to the traffic lights. Then, …

2 A: Hello. Do you know what time the bank opens?
  B: I'm not sure. I'll just ask someone.

3 A: Do you want us to bring anything?
  B: That would be great. Could you bring some salad, and maybe something for dessert?
  A: Yes, of course. Anything else?
  B: No, that'll be fine.

4 A: Could you help me with my bags?
  B: I'm sorry, I can't. I've got my hands full.

5 A: Would you mind opening the door for me?
  B: Of course not. There you are.
  A: Thank you. That's very kind.

6 A: Could you tell me what time the show starts?
  B: Let me have a look. The afternoon show starts at 3p.m.
  A: Thanks very much.

7 A: Would you mind coming to get me from the station?
  B: OK. Sure. Wait outside and I'll be there in ten minutes.

8 A: Do you know if there's a post office near here?
  B: Yes, there is – there's one just along this road.

UNIT 6 Recording 1

1 If I had more time, I'd learn to ski.
2 If you didn't work, what would you do?
3 If they had to move, they wouldn't live with me.
4 She'd go out at night if her parents let her.
5 Where would you go if you had the chance?
6 I wouldn't sleep if I drank that coffee.

UNIT 6 Recording 2

In the eyes of street criminals, everybody communicates something. Some people communicate strength and power; others communicate 'I am a victim'. Researchers Jean A. Hampton and Robert Ealey asked convicted criminals to watch a secret video of a street scene and then say which people look like possible victims of a crime. They did it easily. The potential victims, surprisingly, were not always small women; sometimes they were big men. For this interview, Robert Ealey looked at this picture of a street scene and explained which people were potential victims.

UNIT 6 Recording 3

I = Interviewer   E = Robert Ealey

I: So which of these people would a criminal go for?
E: Not the ones you think.
I: Can you explain?
E: Yeah, so for example, you've got an old woman, see?
I: Yes.
E: So you're a criminal, OK? You might think, OK, this old woman is small and weak. She's not going to fight me or give me any trouble. But who's she with?
I: She's with a dog.
E: That's right. And the thing about dogs is they are unpredictable. And the last thing you want if you're a criminal is unpredictability. You have about five seconds maximum to commit the crime and you don't want any surprises. OK? So you leave the old woman.
I: Right. Is that really the length of time for a street crime?
E: Five seconds? That's the maximum. Most street crimes take maybe two seconds, then it's over.
I: Wow.
E: OK, so let's take someone else. There's a woman talking into a mobile phone, OK?
I: Yes, I see her.
E: Easy victim or not?
I: Well, if she's talking on a mobile phone, she could tell her friend what's happening, right?
E: And then what?
I: Um, the friend calls the police?
E: And do you think the police are going to get there in five seconds?
I: Well, no.
E: No, this woman on the phone is a potential victim. The phone doesn't matter. The reason she's a potential victim is that she isn't paying attention to what's happening around her. She isn't looking at other people. She's distracted.
I: I see.
E: The same with the tourists looking at the map, OK?

I: Right.
E: They're concentrating on the map, not the people around them. This also tells the criminal that these people are lost and don't know what they're doing.
I: But there are two of them, right, so maybe a criminal would hesitate?
E: Maybe, but don't forget, it takes half a second to steal something and run. OK, what about the man at the cashpoint?
I: The guy taking cash out of the bank?
E: What's he doing wrong?
I: Well, if that was me, the cash would be in my wallet before I turned round.
E: That's right. He's basically saying, 'look at me, I've just taken out lots of money and I'm too stupid to put it in my wallet quickly'. He's a criminal's dream. What about the woman in a mini-skirt?
I: Well, she's attractive and … I don't know. She's not exactly big and strong either. Maybe a victim?
E: But look at her body language. She's confident, she knows where she's going, she's looking straight ahead and she's probably moving fast. No criminal would go for her.
I: That's interesting. So body language is pretty important.
E: It's extremely important. Look at the man in the coat. Big man, probably strong, but what's his body telling us?
I: He's not focusing.
E: Yes, that's right. He's looking at his feet. He doesn't know who's around him. Any criminal will think, 'nice coat, probably a fat wallet in there, full of money, and he's not concentrating'. The key for a street criminal is surprise. It doesn't matter who the victim is; if you can surprise them, they have no chance.
I: The couple leaving the taxi?
E: Rule number one of the street: if you have anything valuable, don't show it. This man's wearing an expensive watch which everyone can see. The other thing is people leaving cars are always in a weak position. They aren't standing up properly and they aren't aware of who else is on the street.

UNIT 6   Recording 4

Conversation 1
A: Bad news, I'm afraid.
B: What's the matter?
A: I'm afraid it needs a new engine.

Conversation 2
A: What's the problem?
B: I'm sorry to have to tell you, but we lost the match.

Conversation 3
A: I've got some good news for you.
B: What's that?
A: We've won a holiday for two in Turkey!

Conversation 4
A: I'm afraid I've got some bad news.
B: What's happened?
A: The flight's been cancelled.

Conversation 5
A: There's something I've got to tell you.
B: What's that?
A: I failed my exam.

Conversation 6
A: You'll never guess what happened.
B: What?
A: I was promoted!

Conversation 7
A: Unfortunately, we were burgled last night.
B: Oh no. That's terrible.

Conversation 8
A: I've got something to tell you.
B: What is it?
A: We're getting married.

UNIT 7   Recording 1

1 He's very gifted.
   She's really skilful.
2 He has an aptitude for sport.
   I'm hopeless at gymnastics.
3 He thinks he's useless.
   She has a talent.
4 They say he's an expert.
   She has great ability.

UNIT 7   Recording 2

A: Sidis was the greatest genius in history.
B: William Sidis? A genius.
C: Probably the greatest mind of the twentieth century.
D: They say his IQ was between 250 and 300. That's off the scale.
E: A genius.
F: William Sidis? Great brain, difficult life.
G: Sidis? Genius.

Was William Sidis the most intelligent man who ever lived? If so, why isn't he famous? Why isn't his name known like the names of Einstein, Leonardo and Charles Darwin? What can his life teach us?

William James Sidis was born on April 1st in 1898. That's right: April the first, April Fool's Day. His parents were Boris and Sarah Sidis, Russian–Jewish immigrants who had settled in New York. They were both passionately interested in education. Boris was a psychologist who taught at Harvard University and Sarah used to read Greek myths to her son as bedtime stories.

It soon became clear that their son was something special. Aged six months, William said his first word: 'door'. At seven months, he pointed at the moon and said 'moon'. At eighteen months, William could read *The New York Times*. And aged three, he reached up to a typewriter and wrote a letter to a shop called Macy's asking them to send him some toys!
At six, he could speak Russian, French, German and Hebrew.

All of this took place at home, but soon he made newspaper headlines. He passed the entrance exam to one of the United States' best universities at the age of eight. Then, aged nine, he gave a lecture on mathematics at Harvard University. Attended by maths professors and graduate students this lecture put Sidis on the map. He began attending Harvard University two years later, at the age of eleven.

Now that he was in the public eye, things began to go wrong for William Sidis. The media was fascinated by him. Journalists followed him around and wrote articles about this young genius. Not surprisingly, Sidis began to feel like an animal in a zoo, with everyone watching him.

He wasn't interested in becoming famous, nor in becoming an academic. He just wanted to live a quiet, private life. He tried. He went from job to job, publishing only one book of any academic interest. But everywhere he went, whatever he did, people eventually learned who he was and the press kept writing about him. In 1944, he died aged 46, almost forgotten.

Since his death, many stories have been told about Sidis. Some said that his genius burned out like an old light bulb. His sister said Sidis knew all the languages of the world and that he could learn a language in a day. None of this was true. Even his IQ – which was supposed to be between 250 and 300 – was just a guess. No intelligence test has been invented to go to that level of genius.

So what can we learn from his life? Firstly, not all childhood geniuses will produce great things as adults. They may think great thoughts or do incredible calculations, but many of them just do normal jobs and find happiness in that way. Secondly, Sidis spent much of his time and energy running away from fame. Unless they want to be Hollywood stars, people need to be left in peace. That's how most geniuses do great work.

UNIT 7 Recording 3

Conversation 1

A: We really need to stop this. In my view, it's getting out of control. For example, she watched TV for six hours yesterday. Six hours!

B: I must say that's a lot.

A: It *is* a lot. She needs to get out more.

B: And when she's not in front of the TV, she's on the internet.

A: That's what I was saying. She's always in front of a screen.

Conversation 2

A: For me, Elizabeth is the best. She would be really good in this job.

B: Why do you think so?

A: For one thing, she has the right qualifications. For another, she obviously really wants the job.

B: Yeah, that's very clear. I think the other woman …

A: Hayla.

B: Hayla. She would do a good job, too.

A: She would, but having said that, she already has a good job. You can see that Elizabeth is really hungry for this position.

Conversation 3

A = Presenter B = Mr Dyson

A: Mr Dyson, in your presentation you said that the arts in many schools weren't getting enough attention. Can you explain?

B: Yes, the reason I say this is that funding has been cut for arts subjects. There just isn't enough money. Let me give you an example. A school I visited last month wanted to do a play in the little school theatre but there was no money for costumes, for music. So in the end there was no school play and the theatre was closed for the whole summer term.

A: And this is a money issue?

B: I do think we could solve a lot of the problems if the government recognised the arts as it recognises maths or science or reading, yes. Like I said, money isn't everything, but it's part of the problem.

UNIT 8 Recording 1

Elise

E = Elise   I = Interviewer

E: I live next door to my parents, who are on one side, and my brother's family, who are on the other side.

I: Right.

E: It's really, really useful. They're the perfect neighbours.

I: In what sense?

E: Well, I like the situation because we help each other. For example, if I need a babysitter for my kids, it's no problem.

I: And you see each other a lot?

E: We work together in the family business so we see each other every day. And I guess the whole extended family, which is eleven of us including the children, we eat together maybe once or twice a week, always on Sundays and sometimes during the week. So, yes, we do see each other a lot.

I: You never get fed up with the family?

E: No, I think this situation is quite normal in a lot of countries, maybe like Italy. It certainly is for our family. We've always lived in the same town. I've lived here all my life, and we always wanted to live side by side. I hope our children continue the business and live here, too.

I: And what about your husband? Does he like being so close to your family?

E: Um, I've never asked him actually! Yeah, course he does! I think.

Marc

M = Marc I = Interviewer

M: We don't have any neighbours. Our nearest neighbours are a couple of cows that live in a field about ten miles away.

I: Are they good neighbours?

M: Fantastic! Very quiet! No, we really are completely isolated.

I: So how come? I mean, was this your dream?

M: Well, it wasn't at first. We were living in Paris, which is a great city, but it's kind of big and we got tired of crowds of people and all the noise and using public transport. So about ten years ago, we bought an old farmhouse in the middle of nowhere. It's not a functioning farm but it has an internet connection and me and my wife both work online. And we just love the peace and quiet.

I: So the cows aren't yours?

M: No, they belong to a farmer about ten miles away!

I: And isn't it a bit lonely out here?

M: We love it. We never see our neighbours, apart from the cows, which is just fantastic for us as we're a bit antisocial. Actually, you're the first person we've seen this year!

I: Oh, sorry to interrupt your peace!

M: Not a problem. Just don't stay too long!

UNIT 8 **Recording 2**

1 traffic lights
2 high street
3 housing estate
4 sports centre
5 industrial estate
6 car park
7 supermarket
8 language school
9 shopping centre
10 one-way street
11 terraced houses
12 outdoor market
13 gift shop
14 primary school

UNIT 8 **Recording 3**

1 The website which we built is too slow.
2 Those people who are always working don't enjoy life.
3 The ratings site, which I check every day, is growing fast.
4 Those students who do online courses love studying.
5 Near my flat, where you're staying, there's a supermarket.

UNIT 9 **Recording 1**

1 If I'd known you were coming, I would've waited.
2 If I'd waited, I would've been late.
3 If I'd been late, I would've missed the show.
4 If I'd missed the show, I would've wasted my money.
5 If I'd wasted my money, I would've been angry.

UNIT 9 **Recording 2**

Hello, and welcome to 'Fascinating Facts!' Today we're going to take a look at some of those 'modern' inventions which turn out to be … well, not quite so modern at all!

Let's start with toothpaste. So you think, 'hmm, toothpaste – when was that invented?' A hundred years ago? Maybe two hundred? But we find that actually, toothpaste has been around for sixteen hundred years. People from Egypt used it and then the Ancient Greeks and Romans used it. Was it the same as modern toothpaste? Definitely not. Ancient Greek toothpaste used ingredients like crushed bones and oyster shells.

OK, another invention for you: biological weapons. Again, you think, 'biological weapons – must be a twentieth-century invention'. Wrong again. Biological weapons have been used for over three thousand years. Probably beginning in Ancient Greece, it was common for one side to poison their enemy's water supply during a war. Some generals would even throw dead bodies at the enemy or into the enemy's river. One leader called Hannibal even put poisonous snakes into pots and threw them onto an enemy's ship. In the eighteenth century, one way American Indians were killed was through using infected blankets given to them by the Europeans who were colonising America.

Next topic: football. Just how old is the game? The answer is, we don't really know. But we do know that forms of it were played in China over two thousand years ago. And it also seems that the game developed by chance in different parts of the world. Wherever European explorers went, they discovered that native people already played some kind of football: Aborigines in Australia, the Inuit in Greenland, Japan and the Americas. So I suppose it really is the people's game.

Right. Central heating. It's been a wonderful thing for us in cold countries and helps us get through the winters. But most of us don't realise it's a very old invention. Once again, the Ancient Greeks were the first in Europe, over two thousand years ago, although there was a similar system in Korea. Both of these civilisations had pipes and controlled fires under the floors to keep the buildings warm. In England, one of the first examples of central heating was in the 1830s. A rich banker installed it in his house so that he could grow grapes in England's cold weather!

The final invention we're going to look at today is the good old umbrella. If we look at a number of ancient sculptures from Egypt and Persia, which is now called Iran, it's clear that the umbrella has been around for a long, long time, certainly more than two thousand years. Interestingly, it seems that only kings or very important people had umbrellas in these sculptures. So they were a symbol of high social class. But what were they for? In Europe we tend to think of umbrellas as things to protect us from the rain. But historically, they protected people from the sun. And later, they became a fashion item.

UNIT 9 **Recording 3**

1 The Institute is given a million euros a year.
2 One day a cure for cancer 'll be discovered.
3 The files were stolen last year.
4 These photos were taken at the end of the war.
5 The missing people have been found.
6 The paintings are cleaned once a year.

UNIT 9 **Recording 4**

1 A: Marisa had her baby yesterday.
   B: Did she? What wonderful news!
2 A: I'm doing an online project about *Minecraft*.
   B: Oh really? That's interesting.
3 A: His cousin was an Olympic boxer.
   B: Was he? Wow!
4 A: My sister doesn't eat meat.
   B: Doesn't she? OK, I'll cook fish.
5 A: I think we need to go down this road here.
   B: That's right! I remember that café.
6 A: I love Lady Gaga!
   B: Do you? I think she's crazy.
7 A: Did you know that dolphins have names for each other.
   B: That's interesting.
8 A: My parents have never been here.
   B: Haven't they? When are they going to visit?
9 A: Jake was the number one student in the country.
   B: Really? I didn't know that.
10 A: John's got the car. We'll have to travel by bus.
   B: Will we? Oh, that's annoying.

UNIT 10 Recording 1

P = Presenter, A = Amy, J = Jay-Jay

P: In 2007, one city decided to take a stand against climate change. 2.2 million people across Sydney switched off their lights for an event that would become known across the world as Earth Hour. Earth Hour quickly went global, spreading across the world, and in 2010, thousands of cities in 128 countries took part. Global landmarks like the Eiffel Tower in Paris, the Egyptian Pyramids, New York's Empire State Building and Sydney Harbour Bridge all plunged into darkness as millions of people around the world switched their lights off to protest against climate change.

Organisers say that they want to demonstrate what people can do to reduce their carbon footprint and save energy, and thus draw attention to the problem of climate change. However, critics describe the event as meaningless. In today's programme, we're asking what you think. Can Earth Hour really make a difference? Is it a good way to raise awareness about the problems the world is facing? Have you taken part in the switch-off? First on the line, we have Amy. Amy, can you tell us what you think?

A: I think Earth Hour is a great idea. It's a really simple way for people to show that they care about the environment and want something to change.

P: So, did you do anything for Earth Hour last year, Amy?

A: Yes, I did. I was at home with my two children, who are eight and thirteen years old, and we switched the lights off at home and had our dinner by candlelight.

P: And how did you find that? What did the children think?

A: It was brilliant. The children loved it and we enjoyed a really quiet hour, with no television or music. We talked, actually. And we'll be doing it again this year, definitely.

P: Thank you, Amy. Thanks for calling. Now, we've got Jay-Jay on the line. Jay-Jay, what do you think of Earth Hour?

J: I think it's a complete waste of time. I can't believe it.

P: Wow. And why is that, Jay-Jay? What's the problem?

J: I don't understand how anybody can think that turning off your lights for one hour is really going to make any difference. It's just a way for people to do something which makes them feel better. They turn their lights off for an hour and then they think they've done something about climate change. And then they can carry on as they were before. What we need is for people to really change how they behave every day, not just for an hour. They need to use less electricity, not drive around in their cars everywhere. We need governments to make big changes and turning your lights off … well, it's just silly.

P: But don't you think, Jay-Jay, that it is a symbol, a gesture that helps to get people around the world thinking about the problems?

J: Yes, you're right. But the main problem is not to get people thinking about it, but to get people to actually change the way that they live, and that's not easy.

P: You're right about that. I suppose …

UNIT 10 Recording 2

1 Gina refused to come with us.
2 He promised to call me later.
3 They decided to go out for a meal.
4 They agreed not to go on holiday this year.
5 She warned us that the restaurant was very expensive.
6 They invited James to go to the theatre with them on Friday.
7 The teacher explained that the children grow vegetables in the garden.
8 He recommended buying our fruit at the market.

ANSWER KEY

UNIT 1

1.1

1A

2 fluency
3 mother tongue
4 foreign
5 native speaker
6 slang
7 jargon
8 learning strategies
9 skill
10 accuracy

B

2 fluent
3 accurately
4 mother tongue
5 foreigner
6 slang
7 skills
8 native speaker

2A

1 b 2 b 3 b 4 b 5 a 6 a 7 b

B

b 5 c 7 d 1 e 6 f 3 g 4

3A

1 When's the best time to learn a language?
2 Who taught you English first?
3 Where's the dictionary?
4 Why did people stop speaking Latin every day?
5 What did you learn last lesson?
6 What does your name mean?

4A

Maria
Which?   English
How?   In lessons at school
Ahmed
Which?   Dutch
How?   In evening classes (at college in the Netherlands)
Jessie
Which?   Japanese
How?   In day-to-day life informally

B

1 Thailand
2 A translator
3 The Netherlands
4 He spoke English.
5 Because English is commonly used and they don't feel pressure to learn another language.
6 Japan

C

1 d 2 a 3 f 4 c 5 b 6 e

5A

Email 2 needs to be formal.

B

1 Hi Pilar
2 How are you?
3 thought I'd
4 really like
5 can't wait to stay
6 Hope
7 Dear members
8 I am writing to introduce myself
9 I would like to take this opportunity
10 I will explain
11 I look forward to working with you all
12 Yours sincerely

1.2

1A

1 employee, boss
2 classmate, pupil
3 fiancée, fiancé, godfather, godmother
4 team-mate, member

B

1 fiancée
2 classmate
3 boss
4 member
5 pupil
6 employee
7 godfather
8 team-mate

2A

1 emplo**yee**
2 **ment**or
3 **pup**ils
4 **team**-mates
5 fi**anc**ée
6 **part**ner
7 **god**mother
8 **mem**bers

3

1 are, found
2 won, was sleeping
3 don't like, didn't (you) tell
4 Did (you) hear, were driving
5 Do (you) need, 'm staying
6 'm reading, didn't finish
7 get up, leave
8 're waiting, was looking

4

2 a) ii   b) i
3 a) i   b) ii
4 a) ii   b) i
5 a) ii   b) i

5A

1 men – said by women
2 men – said by women
3 women – said by women
4 women – said by women

C

2 Mai
3 Guy
4 Sergio
5 Linda
6 Avril

D

1 spatial perception
2 equip
3 further
4 distantly
5 instincts

6

2 go
3 take
4 do
5 do
6 get
7 go
8 do
9 take
10 get
11 take
12 go

1.3

1

1 d 2 g 3 e 4 h 5 f 6 c 7 b 8 a

2A

Conversation 1
Could I ask a question?
In my opinion
Conversation 2
There are a couple of things I'd like to ask about.
For me, the most important thing
Conversation 3
I have a query.
One thing I'd like to say is that
Conversation 4
Can I ask you about that?
I'd have to say

B

A 4 B 1 C 2 D 3

3

1 a 2 b 3 c 4 c 5 a 6 a 7 c
8 c 9 b

UNIT 2

2.1

1A

1 Crime, thriller
2 biopic
3 fantasy
4 period drama
5 romantic comedy
6 adventure
7 disaster
8 action
9 docudrama

B

1 romantic comedy
2 disaster
3 biopic
4 fantasy
5 action / thriller
6 crime

2
1 've never been, went
2 have you acted, 've acted
3 has travelled, has he visited
4 has won, won
5 lived, did they move
6 Have you been, arrived
7 've been married, met
8 Did you enjoy, haven't had

3
2 's / has been
3 've / have worked
4 've / have lived in
5 've / have been to London

4A
1 we've visited
2 we haven't had
3 we found
4 've left
5 we've already
6 we've had

5
1 at
2 in
3 on
4 at
5 on
6 In
7 by
8 in
9 in
10 by
11 on
12 on

6A/B
1 T
2 F (He was twenty-four years old.)
3 F (He wasn't speeding at the time of the accident.)
4 F (He had a motorcycle accident and lost two teeth.)
5 F (His favourite drink was coffee.)

C
1 b 2 c 3 a 4 c

D
1 barely out of their teens
2 immortalised
3 rebellious attitude
4 a lasting impression
5 assumed

2.2

1A
1 T 2 F

B
A 3 B 4 C 1 D 2

C
1 Rob
2 Gino
3 Danny, a friend
4 people outside the station
5 Marianne
6 John Lennon

2
1 b 2 a 3 a 4 b 5 a 6 a

3
1 happened
2 waited
3 didn't come
4 was driving
5 broke
6 had run out
7 Did (you) enjoy
8 hated
9 had booked
10 hadn't realised / didn't realise
11 were coming
12 was pouring
13 spilled
14 ordered
15 had said / said
16 arrived
17 tasted

4A
1 crash
2 earthquake
3 hostages
4 floods
5 Fugitive
6 demonstration
7 attacked
8 strikes

B
1 a 2 b 3 b 4 a 5 a

5A
Report A
a 2 b 3 c 1
Report B
a 3 b 2 c 1
Report C
a 3 b 2 c 1

B
Report A
1 A priest installed an electronic fingerprint reader in his church.
2 Warsaw, Poland
3 He wants to monitor whether the children attend mass or not.
Report B
1 There was a 'Love Message Yelling Event'.
2 Hibiya Park in central Tokyo, Japan
3 Kiyotaka Yamana started the event after his own marriage failed, to encourage people to be more romantic.
Report C
1 More than a thousand tourists had to be evacuated from Machu Picchu in helicopters.
2 Machu Picchu, Peru
3 The ruins had been cut off by floods and mudslides.

C
1 as soon as
2 During
3 While
4 Until
5 During
6 by the time
7 until

2.3

1
1 told
2 say
3 told
4 told
5 say
6 said

2
1 This happened when
2 Well
3 so
4 Anyway
5 Before long
6 The next thing I knew
7 In the end
8 Anyway

3
1 happened
2 no
3 kidding
4 what
5 then
6 Oh
7 Really
8 amazing

REVIEW 1

1
1 slang
2 native speaker
3 accuracy
4 bilingual
5 foreign
6 fluency

2A
1 do you work for
2 do you do
3 do you deal with
4 did you start
5 Do you enjoy
6 did you apply

3A/B
1 boss
2 classmate
3 team-mate
4 mentor
5 employee
6 partner

4
1 'm
2 'm taking
3 didn't start
4 love
5 saw
6 was looking
7 was reading
8 jumped
9 isn't
10 wanted

5
2 took, took
3 did, went
4 do, take
5 take, go
6 went, got

6
1 c 2 b 3 a 4 c 5 a 6 c

7
3 but
4 ✔
5 am
6 ✔
7 to
8 It's
9 ✔
10 really
11 the (my opinion)
12 for
13 ✔
14 ✔

8
1 You're welcome
2 No problem
3 Of course
4 You're correct
5 Go ahead
6 I see
7 That's right
8 I understand
9 Please continue

9
1 biopic, strike
2 thriller, fugitive
3 comedy, crash
4 science, attack
5 fantasy, earthquake
6 disaster, violent
7 period, demonstrations

10
1 fell
4 did you go
7 didn't sell

11
1 b 2 a 3 a 4 b 5 b 6 a

12
1 for
2 by
3 in
4 on
5 on
6 at
7 on
8 in
9 in
10 on
11 by
12 By
13 on
14 by
15 in

13
1 stayed
2 had left
3 was listening
4 was wearing
5 hadn't turned on
6 didn't finish
7 hadn't been
8 opened
9 were doing
10 didn't eat

14A
1 tell
2 say
3 tell
4 say
5 tell
6 say

B
1 told stories
2 tell jokes
3 said sorry
4 says 'hello'
5 told a white lie
6 say what you mean

15
1 This happened
2 happened
3 Anyway
4 In
5 Oh no
6 Well
7 before
8 So
9 did you do
10 Finally
11 The next thing
12 Oh dear
13 a sudden
14 happened then
15 in
16 funny

CHECK
1 b 2 c 3 c 4 a 5 b 6 a 7 b
8 c 9 c 10 b 11 a 12 c 13 c
14 a 15 b 16 b 17 c 18 b 19 a
20 b 21 a 22 c 23 b 24 c 25 c
26 a 27 c 28 b 29 c 30 b

UNIT 3

3.1

1A
1 e 2 a 3 c 4 b 5 d

B
1 1, waste
2 4, ahead
3 3, multitasking
4 2, prioritising
5 5, leave

2A
1 Kieron
2 Amber
3 Ruth

B
1 c 2 a 3 c 4 b 5 c 6 c

C
1 e 2 a 3 d 4 b 5 c

3
1 Are you going
2 're going
3 are you going
4 'm going to have
5 might
6 'll give
7 Are you doing
8 'll spend

4
1 Are you doing
2 are going out
3 might try / are going to try
4 're/are meeting / 're/are going to meet
5 'll / will be
6 're / are going to be
7 is playing
8 might go
9 'll / will call

5A
1 a 2 b 3 b 4 b 5 a 6 b

6A
1 d 2 c 3 f 4 b 5 a 6 e

B
1 **I've** gone to lunch. **I'll be** back soon.
2 Mr Jackson called (**earlier**). **He didn't leave a** message. (**He said that**) He will call again later.
3 **My** dentist appointment **has been** cancelled. I need to rebook.
4 **I'm** at the cinema. **Your** dinner **is** in the oven. **I'll** see you later.
5 **I'm** going (**to go**) swimming after school – **do you** want to come (**with me**)?
6 **I'm** sorry, I didn't tidy **my** bedroom – **I** was late for school.

3.2

1

c

2

1 Mars and beyond
2 clean energy
3 via phone apps
4 project 3D images
5 They can be used to repair wounds.
6 They think money should be spent on improving the world not on space travel.

3

1 e 2 d 3 a 4 c 5 b

4

1 significant
2 sophisticated
3 wound
4 exploration

5A

2 term
3 short
4 in
5 time
6 next

B

1, 3, 4 and 6 are about things that will happen soon.
2 and 5 are about things that will happen more than three years in the future.

6

2 will you stay
3 you going to speak to Ted tomorrow
4 is unlikely to pass her exam
5 going to be a storm
6 could become the champion
7 are likely to find a cure for cancer one day
8 may not be able to attend the meeting
9 won't have time to go shopping
10 could meet next week

7

1 are
2 be
3 won't
4 to
5 to
6 be / become
7 will
8 are

8

1 foot
2 tea
3 heart
4 rat
5 eye
6 working
7 run
8 hit
9 piece
10 hot
11 face
12 hand

3.3

1

1 it was the wrong number
2 I didn't realise
3 he got the wrong date / the date wrong
4 I didn't recognise your voice
5 it was a different person

2

A 3 B 2 C 1

3

1 Can
2 again
3 repeat
4 What
5 mean
6 say
7 catch
8 get
9 saying

4

1 So you're saying we can't come in.
2 Didn't you say it starts at ten o'clock?
3 So what you mean is we failed.
4 Do you mean to tell me that it costs €50,000?
5 In other words, we are the champions.

UNIT 4

4.1

1A

1 good communicator
2 hard-working
3 ambitious
4 good leader
5 competitive
6 indecisive
7 outside the box
8 motivated
9 risk taker

B

2 competitive
3 hard-working
4 thinks outside the box
5 good communicator
6 good leader
7 risk taker
8 ambitious

2

1 e, don't have to
2 i, shouldn't
3 b, should
4 g, mustn't
5 a, should
6 j, have to
7 d, mustn't
8 h, must
9 c, don't have to
10 f, must

3

2 I've finished this exercise. What ~~I should~~ **should I** do now?
3 The clients don't ~~has~~ **have** to come to the office. We can meet them at the restaurant.
4 I shouldn't ~~to~~ tell you this, but the boss is leaving on Monday.
5 Do we have **to** wear a uniform?
6 Everybody must ~~leaving~~ **leave** the building by 6p.m.
7 She ~~have~~ **has** to be at work by 7.30a.m.
8 I think you should ~~to~~ check what time the film starts.
9 You ~~don't must~~ **mustn't** use a mobile phone in the classroom.
10 We have **to** wait until the IT man comes to fix the system.

4B

A 3 B 1 C 6 D 5 E 4 F 2

C

1 2 2 4 3 4 4 5 5 6 6 1 7 1 8 3

5A

1 listen, leave
2 remind, remember
3 fun
4 job
5 work, forget
6 hear, funny

B

1 remind
2 hear
3 job
4 forget
5 work, fun
6 funny

4.2

1B

1 good salary, beachside mansion, fantastic views of the ocean
2 Because Ben was too busy and there wasn't much time to relax.
3 He was stung by a deadly jellyfish.
4 He is planning to write a book about his experiences, and he might accept a new contract with Tourism Queensland.

2

2, 4, 5 and 9

3

1 a beachside mansion
2 a busy schedule
3 press conferences
4 administrative duties
5 tweeted
6 get the chance
7 rushed
8 immensely

4

1 **a)** brilliant   **b)** boiling
2 **a)** terrible   **b)** furious
3 **a)** tiny   **b)** delicious
4 **a)** impossible   **b)** exhausted
5 **a)** fascinating   **b)** enormous

5

1 to
2 used
3 would
4 used
5 used
6 would
7 use
8 used

6A

1 Did you use to spend your holidays by the sea?
2 We didn't use to have a dog when I was a child.
3 I used to love reading in the evening, but now I'm too tired.
4 I remember how I used to sit in my grandfather's studio and watch him paint.
5 Children always used to play around on the streets in the old days, but there's nobody here now.
6 They used to live in a big house, but they had to move.

B

Sentences 1, 4, 5

7A

1 /s/ 2 /z/ 3 /s/ 4 /s/
5 /z/ 6 /z/ 7 /s/ 8 /s/

8A

2 I am writing to you about …
3 I am currently studying English …
4 I believe that my communication skills, …
5 Thank you for your consideration. If you require …
6 Yours sincerely,
7 Vinnie Jessop

B

1 at your earliest convenience
2 I believe I meet all the requirements of the post
3 proven ability at
4 hands-on
5 regarding
6 I would like to submit an application

4.3

1A

1 a 2 c 3 a 4 a 5 b 6 c 7 b 8 c

B

1 compete
2 salary
3 runs
4 fired
5 interview
6 work

2

1 see things
2 that's a good idea
3 suggest we think about
4 That's fine
5 not sure that I agree
6 see what you mean
7 How about if we

3

1 on
2 all
3 on
4 recap
5 to
6 up

REVIEW 2

1

1 a 2 c 3 a 4 a 5 b 6 a 7 b 8 c

2A

2 last
3 of
4 gets
5 time
6 get
7 distracted
8 use
9 multitask
10 prioritise

B

1 year
2 term
3 long
4 short
5 years'
6 Next

3

1 are going to
2 might not
3 may
4 is going to
5 is likely to
6 will
7 won't
8 may
9 are going to
10 might

4

1 a piece of cake
2 in hot water
3 my foot in it
4 close to my heart
5 the rat race
6 give me a hand
7 Let's face it
8 my cup of tea
9 keep an eye on
10 run out of time

5

1 catch
2 lost
3 get
4 exactly
5 mean
6 say
7 repeat
8 saying
9 what
10 other

6

1 competitive
2 leader
3 amazing
4 exhausted
5 risk taker
6 freezing
7 fascinating
8 salary
9 boss, fired
10 interview
11 furious
12 hard-working

7A

oOo: successful, delicious, exhausted
Ooo: interview, furious, difficult
Oo: tasty, leader, boiling, freezing
oOoo: competitive, impossible

8

1 has to
2 should
3 mustn't
4 don't have to
5 must / have to
6 mustn't
7 must / have to
8 have to
9 shouldn't
10 don't have to

9

1 remember
2 forgotten
3 left
4 listen
5 hear
6 remind
7 funny
8 fun

10A

1 used to live
2 used to work
3 used to study
4 used to have
5 would play
6 would enjoy

B

1 didn't use to have
2 didn't use to work
3 used to enjoy
4 didn't use to wear
5 didn't use to stay
6 would eat

11A

1 that
2 me
3 agree
4 should
5 things
6 don't
7 point
8 about
9 sure
10 suggest
11 What
12 need

B

opinions: I feel that, I think we should think about, The way I see things, Why don't we, How about if we, I suggest we focus on, How about, I think we need to focus on
responses: That's OK by me, I'm not sure that I agree, That's a good point, I'm not sure that's a good idea

CHECK

1 b   2 b   3 a   4 c   5 b   6 c   7 b
8 a   9 b   10 c   11 b   12 a   13 c
14 c   15 a   16 b   17 c   18 b   19 a
20 c   21 c   22 b   23 a   24 c   25 a
26 c   27 a   28 b   29 c   30 a

UNIT 5

5.1

1A

1 T   2 O   3 M

B

1 a   2 c   3 b   4 c   5 a   6 b

2

1 more expensive than
2 better
3 easier
4 bigger
5 heavier
6 the lightest
7 smaller
8 cheaper

3

1 much
2 a little bit
3 by far
4 a lot
5 a bit
6 slightly

4A

1 vaccinations
2 electricity
3 nuclear power
4 computer network
5 antibiotics
6 space travel
7 motorbikes

B

1 genetic engineering
2 nuclear power
3 antibiotics
4 electricity
5 space travel
6 communications satellites
7 solar power
8 vaccination

5A

/ei/ **make:** communications, aeroplanes, vaccinations
/æ/ **apple:** travel, satellites, vacuum
/ə/ **polar:** nuclear, machine, commercial, solar

6A

1 ✔   2 ✘   3 ✔   4 ✘   5 ✘   6 ✔

B

Plan B is better because it is more clearly organised into advantages and disadvantages. The paragraphs are planned and there is an introduction and a conclusion.

C

However, there are also disadvantages. **One of the main advantages is that** when you study online, you …
The problem is that when you study online, there is … students. **Another disadvantage is** you might find it difficult … your studies. **And another thing,** you might experience …
In my opinion, online courses offer students more choice and flexibility. **However,** they are …

5.2

1

Not possible:
2 inquire
3 argue
4 questioned
5 replied
6 quarrelled
7 look into
8 inquires

2

2 question
3 look into
4 debate
5 response
6 investigating
7 inquired
8 reply
9 wondered

3

1 aren't you
2 didn't she
3 have they
4 will he
5 doesn't it
6 did we
7 has it
8 won't you
9 does it
10 didn't you

4

2 was funny, wasn't it
3 won't crash the car, will he
4 wasn't a very good game, was it
5 write to me, won't you
6 didn't miss the last bus, did you
7 speak French, don't you
8 haven't seen my watch, have you

5A

1, 3, and 5 are genuine questions.

6C

1 Which food
2 about stress
3 good for you
4 eat rotting food
5 amount of water turn into ice

D

2 dose
3 smog
4 rotting
5 hatch

7

1 responsible
2 hopeless
3 creative
4 easy
5 effective
6 successful
7 valuable
8 profitable

5.3

1

1 down
2 recharging
3 order
4 fixing
5 switching
6 crashed
7 work
8 sort
9 memory
10 print

2A

A **3** He wants to know if they have to bring anything.

B **4** She wants someone to hold something for her.

C **7** She wants someone to pick her up from the station.

D **2** He wants to know what time the bank opens.

E **1** She wants to know the way to the swimming pool.

F **8** She wants to know if there is a post office near there.

G **6** He wants to know what time the (afternoon) show starts.

H **5** She wants someone to open the door for her.

B

1 could, course
2 know, sure
3 you, of
4 help, sorry
5 opening, not
6 tell, Let
7 mind, Sure
8 if, there

3

1 No, of course not.
2 I'm not sure. Let me have a look.
3 Yes, of course.
4 I'm afraid I can't.
5 Yes, I can.

UNIT 6

6.1

1A

1 exhausting
2 worried
3 confusing
4 annoyed
5 frightening
6 embarrassed
7 confused
8 relaxing
9 satisfied
10 frightened

B

1 frightened
2 annoyed
3 exhausting
4 satisfied
5 confusing
6 embarrassed
7 worried
8 relaxing

2A/B

Reasons: *You're irritated with someone*, You're frustrated about something, People criticise you.
Consequences: *You start to shout*, You throw things around, You feel tense.
Solutions: You do physical exercise, You try meditation, You distance yourself from the situation.

3

1 increases
2 understand
3 solve
4 situations / things
5 change
6 distance
7 breathing / breaths
8 calmly

4A

1 finds, will / 'll leave
2 will get, works
3 exercise, live
4 leave, will / 'll miss
5 will / 'll start, is
6 is, dance
7 is, eat
8 use, won't get

B

2 specific – first conditional
3 general – zero conditional
4 specific – first conditional
5 specific – first conditional
6 general – zero conditional
7 general – zero conditional
8 specific – first conditional

5

2 If you ~~will~~ go to England, you will improve your English.
3 I'll tell him you called when I ~~will~~ see him.
4 ✔
5 If they arrive early, will you ~~to~~ ask them to wait?
6 If you ~~will~~ come to the party tonight, will you bring a friend?
7 When I go to Krakow, I usually ~~will~~ see my aunt.
8 ✔
9 She will get angry if you ~~will~~ say that!
10 I'll / **will** go to the doctor tomorrow if I feel worse.

6A

1 c **2** c **3** a **4** c **5** b **6** a **7** c **8** b

B

1 down
2 on
3 up
4 off
5 on
6 up
7 off
8 off

6.2

1

1 do, experiments
2 watch, programme
3 get, seat
4 hold, sale
5 jump, queue
6 cut, hair
7 raise money

2

2 If she was fast enough, she would / could play for the team.
3 We could drive to your house if we had a car.
4 My life wouldn't be so easy if I didn't have a supportive family.
5 If I had the money, I would buy that house.
6 I would write to my friends if I wasn't so lazy.
7 If you watered your plants regularly, they wouldn't look dry!
8 They would help in the house if their mother asked them.
9 If I didn't work on Saturdays, I could come to the barbecue.

3

2 had
3 'd / would be
4 'd / would introduce
5 had to
6 'd / would change
7 was
8 'd / would be
9 'd / would make
10 wouldn't let
11 was
12 wouldn't have

4A

1 If I had more time, I'd learn to ski.
2 If you didn't work, what would you do?
3 If they had to move, they wouldn't live with me.
4 She'd go out at night if her parents let her.
5 Where would you go if you had the chance?
6 I wouldn't sleep if I drank that coffee.

5A

The topic is what kind of people are likely to be victims of crime.

B

2, 3, 4, 6 and 7 are potential victims.

D

2 Yes, (because she isn't) paying attention to what's happening around her. She isn't looking at other people.
3 Yes, (because they are concentrating on the map, not) the people around them.
4 Yes, (because he didn't put the money) in his wallet quickly.
5 No, (because of her positive) body language. She's confident, she knows where she's going, she's looking straight ahead, and she's probably moving fast.
6 Yes, (because he's looking at his feet and he doesn't know) who's around him.
7 Yes, (because rule number one of the street is: if you have anything valuable,) don't show it.

6A

Summary c

B

1 D   2 C   3 B   4 A

C

Maybe, It's possible that, probably, in all likelihood, In all probability

6.3

1A

1 pass
2 accident
3 offered
4 place
5 engaged
6 lost
7 failed
8 split
9 won
10 promoted
11 degree
12 bought

B

2 e   3 d   4 a   5 b   6 c

2A

A 4   B 3   C 1   D 8   E 2   F 7   G 6   H 5

B

1 Bad news, ~~as~~ I'm afraid.
2 I'm sorry ~~for~~ to have to tell you, but we lost the match.
3 I've got some good ~~unfortunately~~ news for you.
4 I'm afraid ~~of~~ I've got some bad news.
5 There's something ~~who~~ I've got to tell you.
6 You'll never guess what ~~is~~ happened.
7 ~~It's~~ Unfortunately, we were burgled last night.
8 I've got something ~~for~~ to tell you.

3

1 Congratulations, fantastic
2 terrible, sorry
3 Well done, great news
4 awful
5 Have, lucky
6 shame
7 joking

REVIEW 3

1

1 is slightly warmer
2 are far more expensive than
3 the most delicious meal
4 was a lot easier than
5 the simplest
6 much happier
7 a bit shorter than
8 a worse place than

2

1 electricity
2 vaccination
3 space travel
4 genetic engineering
5 solar panels
6 computer network
7 Nuclear power
8 commercial aeroplanes

3

1 discuss
2 respond
3 look
4 wondering
5 research
6 investigate
7 inquiries
8 debate

4

1 can't we
2 haven't they
3 won't we
4 do you
5 wasn't it
6 didn't you
7 will you
8 have you

5

1 painful
2 homeless
3 responsible
4 creative
5 hopeless
6 effective
7 thankful
8 messy

6

1 The car's broken down.
2 My phone needs recharging.
3 It's out of order.
4 The printer needs fixing.
5 Try switching it off and on again.
6 It keeps making this strange noise.
7 It doesn't work any more.
8 We have to sort it out.

7

1 tell, of course
2 if there's, sure
3 checking, course
4 see, look

8

1 annoyed
2 relaxed
3 confusing
4 satisfied
5 embarrassing
6 exhausted
7 worried
8 frightening

9A

1 I'll call
2 don't
3 is
4 will die
5 I'd
6 didn't
7 would
8 don't
9 live
10 get
11 would
12 had

B

1 b   2 c   3 a   4 a   5 c   6 b   7 a   8 c

10

1 up
2 down
3 on
4 on
5 off
6 on
7 off
8 down
9 off
10 down

11

1 b   2 b   3 b   4 c   5 a   6 c   7 b

12

1 c   2 e   3 a   4 g   5 h   6 b   7 f   8 d

13

1 A: I'm sorry to have to ~~telling~~ tell you, but the train has been cancelled.
B: ~~That~~ That's annoying.
2 A: I've got ~~a~~ some good news for you.
B: ~~Congratulation~~ Congratulations!
3 A: There's something I've got to tell ~~to~~ you.
B: Oh. I'm sorry ~~for~~ to hear that.
4 A: You'll never guess ~~to~~ what.
B: That's ~~so~~ fantastic news!
5 A: ~~Unfortunate~~ Unfortunately, I didn't get the job.
B: That's a real shame.

CHECK

1 a   2 b   3 c   4 c   5 b   6 c   7 b
8 c   9 b   10 a   11 c   12 a   13 c
14 b   15 b   16 c   17 a   18 c   19 a
20 b   21 c   22 b   23 c   24 a   25 b
26 a   27 c   28 b   29 b   30 c

UNIT 7

7.1

1

2 focus on
3 hard at
4 world-class
5 high achiever
6 believe in

3

1 DK   2 T   3 F   4 T   5 F   6 F

4

1 b 2 e 3 c 4 a 5 f 6 d

5

1 've / have been going
2 've / have been waiting
3 haven't been sleeping
4 's / has been crying
5 've / have known
6 've / have been skiing
7 have (they) been living
8 Have (you) been watching, 've / have (really) been enjoying

6

1 has been happening
2 haven't had
3 have been staying
4 has been working
5 've / have been thinking
6 haven't decided
7 've / have been looking
8 have found
9 've / have been working
10 's / has been studying

7A

1 on
2 in
3 to
4 on
5 on
6 for
7 about
8 to

B

1 think about
2 pay attention to
3 depends on
4 pick up on
5 have a talent for
6 have access to
7 succeed in
8 rely on

7.2

1A

1 c 2 a 3 b 4 c 5 a 6 b 7 a 8 c

B

1 hopeless, useless
2 gifted, talented
3 skilful
4 expert
5 have a lot of ability, have an aptitude for

2

1 couldn't
2 manage
3 remember
4 was
5 could
6 to
7 wasn't
8 managed

3

Not possible:
1 didn't manage
2 do able to
3 could
4 can
5 are manage to
6 didn't able to
7 'm not manage to
8 could to
9 Do you can
10 Could you

4A

1 ✔
2 a) 8 syllables   b) 7 syllables
3 ✔
4 a) 6 syllables   b) 7 syllables

5B

A When Sidis was seven months old, he pointed at the moon and said 'moon'.
B At eighteen months, he could read *The New York Times*.
C At six, he could speak Russian, French, German and Hebrew.
D Aged nine, he gave a lecture on mathematics at Harvard University.
E Journalists followed him around and wrote articles about him but he didn't achieve much as an adult.
F He died in 1944, aged 46.

C

1 His parents were originally from Russia. They moved to New York.
2 William's first word was 'door'.
3 William was six when he could speak Russian, French, German and Hebrew.
4 When he was nine, he gave a lecture on mathematics at Harvard University.
5 Two years later, he began attending Harvard University.
6 Journalists 'followed him around'.
7 His sister said he knew all the languages of the world and that he could learn a language in a day.
8 For most of his adult life, Sidis was 'running away' from fame.

6A

1 His first word was *door*, not *moon*. He took one day to learn a language, not one week.
2 Journalists followed him around and wrote articles about this young genius Not all childhood geniuses will produce great things as adults

B

1 Uni (university), yrs (years)
2 &
3 close 2 him
4 THE LIFE OF WILLIAM SIDIS
5 Background
6 leave people alone

7.3

1

1 an MA
2 face-to-face learning
3 an apprenticeship
4 qualifications
5 a certificate
6 a PhD
7 an online course
8 distance learning
9 a driving licence
10 a degree

2A

1 b 2 c 3 c

B

1 a 2 b 3 b 4 b 5 a
6 b 7 b 8 a 9 a 10 b

UNIT 8

8.1

1

2 I am really interested in other people – actually my mum says I am too **nosy about** other people's lives.
3 Whenever they're arguing, I prefer to mind **my own** business.
4 Hayley has invited **us over** for dinner at her house.
5 Those neighbours are **a nuisance** – they're always …
6 She got **to know** her neighbours immediately.
7 Please don't **disturb me**.
8 One thing that gets **on my** nerves is when …
9 Xun hasn't made **friends with** her neighbours yet …
10 I keep myself **to myself**.

2

2 Have you received **the** letter I sent you?
3 ✔
4 Do you have **a** pen I can borrow?
5 ✔
6 Is there **an** airport in the city?
7 I'm going to Germany in **the** morning.
8 We live by **the** Pacific Ocean.
9 My brother is **an** actor.
10 ✔
11 ✔
12 Did you see **the** film I told you about?
13 I live in **the** United States.
14 She's **the** nicest woman I know.
15 ✔

3

2 b, vi There are plenty of good restaurants in the town, especially if you like French food.
3 f, iii I don't know much about this city, but I like the architecture.
4 a, v All of us love this place because it's so friendly.
5 g, vii If you have enough time, go to the museum – it's great.
6 c, viii There are too many cars in most big cities – I hate traffic!
7 e, i I've got lots of friends in this community.
8 h, ii I spent a bit of time in Poland when I was younger.

4

3 but
4 of
5 ✔
6 ✔
7 ✔
8 to (money)
9 small
10 ✔
11 a (five hours)
12 more
13 ✔
14 all
15 ✔
16 ✔
17 a

5A

1 Elise's neighbours are her parents and her brother's family.
 Marc's neighbours are 'a couple of cows' / a farmer.
2 Elise likes this situation because they 'help each other'.
 Marc likes the situation because he and his wife 'just love the peace and quiet'.
3 Elise sees her neighbours every day. They work together and they all eat together once or twice a week.
 Marc never sees his neighbours, apart from the cows.
4 Elise has lived there all her life.
 Marc has lived there for ten years.

B

1 perfect
2 family
3 eleven
4 Sunday
5 normal
6 husband
7 ten
8 Paris
9 transport
10 farmhouse
11 online
12 first

C

1 a 2 b 3 b 4 b 5 b 6 a

6A

2 high street
3 housing estate
4 sports centre
5 industrial estate
6 car park
7 supermarket
8 language school
9 shopping centre
10 one-way street
11 terraced houses
12 outdoor market
13 gift shop
14 primary school

7

1 housing estate
2 language school
3 primary school
4 one-way street
5 sports centre
6 terraced houses
7 traffic lights
8 car park
9 supermarket
10 gift shop
11 outdoor market
12 industrial estate
13 high street
14 shopping centre

8.2

1

2 j 3 f 4 k 5 b 6 l 7 i 8 e
9 h 10 c 11 d 12 g

2

3 a 4 b 5 b 6 a 7 b 8 a

3

1 clothing that
2 place where
3 person who
4 name that
5 which has
6 thing that
7 who behaves
8 place where

4

1 a 2 a 3 b 4 a 5 b

5A

A *silver surfer* is an older person, typically over 50, who uses the internet.

B

1 Her granddaughter, Sonya.
2 She didn't really understand it so she found it annoying.
3 Most people who go online are under 50.
4 Her family live quite far away and she doesn't drive.
5 They tend to use email the most.

C

1 e 2 a 3 c 4 b 5 d

6A

1 feature
2 like
3 would
4 best

B

1 B 2 A 3 D 4 C

8.3

1A

1 help yourself
2 Excuse the mess
3 Make yourself at home
4 Be my guest
5 Have a seat
6 Put your feet up

B

A 2 B 5 C 1 D 3 E 4 F 6

2

1 a 2 b 3 a 4 b 5 b
6 b 7 a 8 b 9 b 10 a

3

1 It's no problem.
2 Not at all.
3 That's all right.
4 It's fine.
5 It's nothing.
6 You really don't have to.

REVIEW 4

1

1 Our company focuses ~~at~~ **on** quality software.
2 ✔
3 It's important that we work ~~hardly~~ **hard** at this.
4 The key is to believe ~~of~~ **in** yourself.
5 ✔
6 We'll improve if we ~~are~~ practise every day.

2

1 known
2 been waiting
3 been reading
4 invited
5 been working
6 been learning
7 seen
8 met

3

1 to
2 to
3 on
4 in
5 for
6 on
7 on
8 about
9 with
10 at / for
11 to
12 to
13 in
14 for
15 in
16 with
17 about
18 for

4

1 Because he's an expert in his subject.
2 Because he has a lot of ability in maths.
3 Because she's gifted at the sport.
4 Because they have a talent for writing scripts.
5 Because he has an aptitude for the game.
6 Because I'm absolutely hopeless at science.

5

1 We can't play
2 She can sing
3 Are you able
4 didn't manage to
5 wasn't able to
6 manage to clean
7 could you speak
8 managed to break

6

1 qualifications
2 licence
3 apprenticeship
4 learning
5 distance
6 online
7 degree
8 Master's

7A

1 view
2 reason
3 For
4 must
5 For
6 another
7 For
8 what
9 said
10 do
11 give
12 said

B

O: 1, 2, 3, 4, 10
E: 5, 6, 7, 11
R: 8, 9, 12

8

2 myself to myself
3 got to know
4 your own business
5 over for dinner
6 get on well

9

2 ✔, ✔
3 ✔, **the** best ones
4 ✔, **the** rat
5 ~~a~~ **the** party, too ~~much~~ **many** people
6 ✔, ~~the~~ **a** haircut
7 ✔, **the** moon
8 too ~~many~~ **much** time, ✔
9 ✔, **a** lot of pepper
10 ✔, ~~the~~ Barcelona

10

2 house
3 calling
4 school
5 apartment
6 news
7 shops
8 flat

11

2 ✔
3 Corporate websites
4 Ratings sites
5 ✔
6 Personal homepages
7 ✔
8 ✔
9 ✔
10 dating sites
11 ✔
12 Blogs

12

1 who I spoke to was very nice
2 which we visited had a wonderful exhibition
3 where she was born is now under water
4 who is in the fashion industry, lives in Paris
5 where I grew up is now a theatre
6 who is my best friend, works with my father
7 which lasted for ten days, is now finished

13

1 have
2 Be
3 Excuse
4 Make
5 put
6 help

14

Conversation 1
Pete: Do I need ~~for~~ to bring anything?
Don: No, it's not ~~the~~ necessary.
Conversation 2
Kat: It's considered ~~be~~ a bit rude.
Conversation 3
Andre: Is this ~~for~~ a bad time?
Bella: Can you ~~to~~ come back in ten minutes?
Andre: I didn't ~~can~~ realise you were in a meeting.
Bella: Don't ~~to~~ worry about it.
Conversation 4
Nick: What should we ~~to~~ do?
Tam: No, you'd better ~~be~~ not.

15

2 B: It's **no** problem. I can photocopy mine.
3 B: That's **all right**. It didn't hurt.
4 B: Not **at** all. We usually don't start till 3.15.
5 B: No, **it's** nothing. I didn't even feel it.
6 B: Honestly, **it's** fine. Don't worry about it.

CHECK

1 b   2 c   3 b   4 a   5 c   6 c   7 c   8 c
9 c   10 a   11 c   12 a   13 b   14 a
15 c   16 b   17 c   18 a   19 a   20 b
21 a   22 b   23 c   24 a   25 c   26 a
27 a   28 c   29 c   30 a

UNIT 9

9.1

1A

1 revolution
2 turning point
3 development
4 spread
5 advance
6 movement
7 invention
8 foundation
9 discovery
10 progress

T	U	R	N	I	N	G	P	O	I	N	T
D	A	E	B	P	R	O	G	R	E	S	S
E	C	V	D	E	R	I	O	M	E	I	P
V	F	O	U	N	D	A	T	I	O	N	T
E	E	L	U	F	C	S	S	G	J	V	E
L	S	U	A	V	U	A	P	L	I	E	D
O	W	T	V	A	P	D	R	A	G	N	E
P	D	I	S	C	O	V	E	R	Y	T	X
M	E	O	R	E	K	A	A	E	I	I	H
E	D	N	I	U	F	N	D	O	E	O	O
N	C	I	N	T	I	C	F	R	S	N	E
T	M	O	V	E	M	E	N	T	C	L	F

B

1 discovery
2 spread
3 development
4 progress
5 advances
6 movement
7 revolution
8 invention

2

1 c   2 c   3 b   4 a   5 c   6 a

3

2 If Archduke Ferdinand hadn't been assassinated, World War I wouldn't have started.
3 If people from Sumer hadn't needed permanent records, they wouldn't have invented writing.
4 If William the Conqueror hadn't invaded England in 1066, the English language wouldn't have changed.
5 If Charles Darwin hadn't travelled to South America, he wouldn't have developed the theory of evolution.
6 If sailors on the *Titanic* had seen the iceberg, 1,595 people wouldn't have died.

4A

2 If I'd waited, I **would've** been late.
3 If I'd been late, I **would've** missed the show.
4 If I'd missed the show I **would've** wasted my money.
5 If I'd wasted my money, I **would've** been angry.

5A

2 Ancient Greece, over 3,000
3 China, over 2,000
4 Ancient Greece / Korea, over 2,000
5 Egypt / Persia (Iran), more than 2,000

B

A Ancient Greek toothpaste used oyster shells.
B Hannibal used snakes as a biological weapon.
C The Inuit played a type of football.
D A rich English banker installed central heating in his house so he could grow grapes.
E In ancient sculptures from Egypt and Persia, only kings or very important people had umbrellas.

C

a) enemy
b) symbol
c) installed
d) infected
e) crushed

6A

b) The History of Writing

B

1 In 3200 BC, Sumerians invented writing.
2 While
3 As a result

9.2

1A/B

Sam is generation Y: she **was ~~been~~ born** in the 1990s and was brought up in a world of social media, technological progress and globalisation. Sam has a university education, a good standard of living and a busy social life. But she is miserable. According to recent research, unhappiness **is ~~be~~ felt** more often by this generation than the previous one. Some of the reasons may seem obvious: for example unemployment and expensive housing are causing pressure for people. Nowadays each graduate-level job (meaning it requires university education) is chased by over 100 people and millennials are much less likely to have their own home than earlier generations. However these are not new problems, such issues have been faced by young people for a long time. Instead some alternative reasons **have ~~be~~ been suggested** by recent research: the first is that generation Y expect more from life than their parents did and are disappointed when they don't get it. While generation X hoped for a secure job, generation Y expect the job to be interesting as well as secure. Secondly, generation Y ~~been~~ **have been told** to believe in themselves, that they deserve success quickly. In the past, years of hard work was seen as normal while generation Y believe they should have a management level job within a few years of starting work.
It is these differences between expectation and real life that make generation Y less happy than their parents. So how can someone in the Y generation be happy? The best way is not to give up dreams but to understand that no job is perfect and any kind of success **will probably only ~~to~~ be achieved** by years of hard work.

2A

2 One day a cure for cancer will/'ll be discovered.
3 The files were stolen last year.
4 These photos were taken at the end of the war.
5 The missing people have been found.
6 The paintings are cleaned once a year.

B

The auxiliary verbs *are*, *were*, *has(n't) been* and *have been* are contracted (said in a shortened way).

3

2 over a quarter-century
3 just over a century ago
4 millennium
5 over seven decades
6 the generation
7 just over a fortnight
8 half a century

4A

1 have
2 make
3 give
4 come
5 have
6 have
7 come
8 give
9 give
10 have
11 come
12 make
13 give
14 make
15 come
16 make

B

1 having trouble, have a break
2 made a decision, made a profit
3 give me a call, give me directions
4 come naturally, came first
5 give a talk, give instructions

5A

1 around 1880–1895
2 1945 to about 1960
3 A novel: *Generation X: Tales for an Accelerated Culture*
4 Rebelling against their parents' values, not wanting to work for the same company their whole life, listening to 'grunge' music, playing video games
5 between 1980s and 1990s
6 Love of technology, amazing networkers, constantly online, great multitaskers

B

1 Socrates say (about the younger generation)
2 begin naming each generation
3 people were killed in World War I
4 after the Second World War (from 1945–1960)
5 wrote *Millennials Rising: The Next Great Generation* / first described Generation Y in detail
6 people used the internet in 2010

C

1 e   2 d   3 c   4 a   5 b   6 f

9.3

1
1 brave
2 charismatic
3 exemplary
4 influential
5 inspirational
6 creative
7 original
8 innovative

2
1 a 2 b 3 b 4 a
5 b 6 a 7 b 8 a

3A
1 Did
2 That
3 Was
4 Doesn't
5 right
6 Do
7 interesting
8 Haven't
9 didn't
10 Will

UNIT 10

10.1

1A
1 on standby
2 double glazed
3 processed
4 insulated
5 organic
6 pre-prepared
7 packaging
8 energy-saving
9 recycled
10 second-hand

B
1 organic
2 second-hand
3 double glazed
4 energy-saving
5 pre-prepared
6 processed
7 recycled
8 standby
9 packaging
10 insulated

2A
1 lights
2 Eiffel Tower
3 Pyramids
4 Sydney
5 change
6 different

3A
1 F (2.2 million people)
2 T
3 T
4 F (Some people think the event is meaningless.)
5 T
6 F (He doesn't think the event helps people to change their behaviour.)

B
1 stand
2 global
3 part
4 plunged
5 attention
6 raise
7 waste

4
1 didn't
2 were
3 had
4 her
5 next
6 his
7 would
8 they

5A
A: I want to go to Spain because I've never been there before.
T: How are you planning to travel?
A: I'm thinking of going by plane.
T: Have you thought about taking the train instead?
A: No, I haven't, but it's a good idea.
T: It's cheaper than flying. I'll show you some of the train routes.
A: OK.
T: Have you decided where you want to stay?
A: No, I haven't. Could you show me what accommodation is available?
T: There's an eco-farm near Valencia where you can stay for free if you help the farmer pick his olives.
A: That sounds great!

B
2 asked her, was planning
3 she was thinking
4 she'd thought
5 she hadn't, it was
6 would show her
7 had decided, she wanted
8 she hadn't
9 could stay, helped
10 sounded great

6
1 misunderstood
2 disobey
3 reuse
4 unusual
5 underestimated
6 disappeared
7 untidy
8 renew
9 unethical
10 disagree

10.2

1
1 c 2 b 3 a 4 c 5 a 6 b 7 c

2
A 4 B 5 C 2 D 1 E 3

3
1 Jorge
2 Irene
3 Claire
4 Claire
5 Mariella
6 Irene

4
1 pleasant
2 water
3 yellow middle
4 soft; liquid
5 pasta
6 sad because you haven't got

5
2 suggested spending
3 invited us to stay
4 offered to take
5 explained that it would be / explained that it was
6 recommended that we travel / recommended travelling
7 agreed to choose
8 warned us not to go
9 promise to write

6A
1 refused to come
2 promised to call
3 decided to go
4 agreed not to go
5 warned us that
6 invited James to go
7 explained that the children
8 recommended buying

B
The words *to*, *for*, *at* and *that* are unstressed.

7A
The writer doesn't recommend the restaurant because they thought the atmosphere was uninviting, the service was poor and the food was not great, either.

B
a so 2
b Although 4
c unless 5
d such, that 3
e While 1

8A
1 no information given
2 no information given
3 ✔
4 ✔
5 ✔

10.3

1

1 passport
2 check in
3 aisle
4 boarding card
5 X-ray machine
6 board
7 priority boarding
8 proceed to gate number
9 hand luggage

2

1 b   2 c   3 a   4 b   5 c   6 b   7 a

3

1 c   2 a   3 f   4 d   5 e   6 b

REVIEW 5

1

1 revolution
2 turning point
3 development
4 spread
5 advance
6 movement
7 invention
8 foundation
9 discovery
10 progress

2

1 hadn't helped, wouldn't have finished
2 would have gone, hadn't rained
3 'd / had studied, wouldn't have failed
4 would have told, 'd / had had
5 hadn't scored, wouldn't have won
6 would you have done, 'd / had missed

3

1 are sold here
2 isn't produced in England
3 is being built
4 was assassinated
5 wasn't written by Samuel Beckett
6 haven't been told anything about the exam

4

1 millennium
2 a decade
3 a fortnight
4 a quarter-century
5 generation
6 the nineties

5

Not possible:
1 well
2 a discussion
3 project
4 homework
5 forward
6 problem
7 money
8 progress

6

1 creative
2 original
3 charismatic
4 exemplary
5 innovative
6 brave
7 inspirational
8 influential

7

2 c, i, I haven't a clue.
3 a, iii, I'm fairly sure it's Jane.
4 f, iv, It's definitely not Sarah.
5 d, ii, I'm sure it isn't Elizabeth.
6 e, vi, I have no idea.

8

1 just about
2 Is
3 interesting
4 couldn't

9

1 organic
2 energy-saving, insulated
3 double glazed, on standby
4 pre-prepared, packaging
5 second-hand, recycled

10

2 you didn't know the answer
3 you had been to Germany
4 you could swim
5 you weren't going to university
6 you would be there on Monday
7 you wouldn't be able to help
8 you hadn't spoken to Kevin

11

1 He asked me when ~~started the game~~ **the game started**.
2 He asked me if I ~~do~~ **play / played** any instruments.
3 ✔
4 ✔
5 He asked me why ~~was I~~ **I was** crying.
6 She asked me if ~~slept my baby~~ **my baby slept** all night.
7 She asked me if they ~~did speak~~ **spoke** English.

12

2 misjudged, overcooked
3 unbelievable, overweight
4 untidy, disobeyed
5 reuse, recycle
6 disapproved, unethical
7 underestimate, renew
8 disappeared, unknown

13

1 David _promised_ (invited) us to his birthday party. _Sentence 6_
2 The tour guide _refused_ (warned) us about poisonous spiders. Sentence 3
3 The doorman _suggested_ (refused) to let me into the club because I was wearing jeans. Sentence 7
4 I _explained_ (offered) to take her for dinner to say 'thank you'. Sentence 5
5 The teacher _invited_ (explained) the grammar clearly so everyone understood. Sentence 1
6 My dad _warned_ (promised) to buy me an ice cream if I behaved well. Sentence 2
7 Minty _offered_ (suggested) going to Greece for our holiday. Sentence 4

14

1 that I
2 that
3 me to
4 me
5 to wait
6 to take
7 to give
8 to move
9 to
10 trying

15

1 d   2 a   3 e   4 g   5 b   6 h   7 c   8 f

16

1 the most important thing is to
2 make sure you bring
3 watch out for snakes
4 it's not very common
5 if I were you, I'd start
6 you need to bring
7 have a tendency to bring
8 Whatever you do, don't pack
9 don't forget to bring
10 on the whole
11 be careful to eat
12 you'd better take some

CHECK

1 a   2 c   3 b   4 c   5 c   6 b   7 a   8 a
9 c   10 c   11 b   12 b   13 c   14 b
15 c   16 a   17 a   18 c   19 b   20 c
21 c   22 a   23 b   24 c   25 a   26 b
27 b   28 a   29 b   30 b

Pearson Education Limited
Edinburgh Gate
Harlow
Essex CM20 2JE
England
and Associated Companies throughout the world.

www.pearsonelt.com

First published 2015
ISBN: 978-1-4479-7686-8

Set in Aptifer sans 10/12 pt
Printed in Slovakia by Neografia

Illustration acknowledgements
195 Eric (kja-artists.com): pp13, 24, 38; 087 Sean (kla-artists.com): pp8, 11, 22, 36, 40,
41, 49, 55, 61

Photo acknowledgements
The publisher would like to thank the following for their kind permission to reproduce
their photographs:

(Key: b-bottom; c-centre; l-left; r-right; t-top)

123RF.com: 24 (A), Antonio Abrignani 66, Dmitry Rukhlenko 4; **Alamy Images:**
Cultura Creative 46c, Danita Delimont 24 (B), Image Source 7, Juice Images 18br,
moodboard 24 (C), Radius Images 24 (D), Alan Wrigley 51b; **Corbis:** Bettmann 10,
Fancy / Randy Faris 23, Retna Ltd / Armando Gallo 64tr, Stew Slavin / Bettmann 34;
Fotolia.com: Alliance 46r; **Getty Images:** Ableimages / Photodisc 39bl, AFP / Kazuhiro
Nogi 64tc, AFP / Torsten Blackwood 25tr, Antony Giblin / Lonely Planet Images 13,
Blend Images / Brand X Pictures 54, Graham Chadwick 64tl, E+ / Isitsharp 18bc,
Glow Images 69t, Hemera / Erwin Purnomosidi 24 (F), Jupiterimages / Creatas 27,
Jupiterimages / Photolibrary 69b, Jupiterimages / Stockbyte 39tr, Photodisc / Nick Daly
39tl, Stock4B 69c, Stockbyte / Jack Hollingsworth 24 (E); **Pearson Education Ltd:**
Studio 8 39br; **Press Association Images:** AP / Brian Cassey 25tl; **Rex Features:** David
Hartley 48tl, Sharok Hatami 48tc, Vitra Haus building, Vitra Design Museum, architects
Herzog & de Meuron, Weil am Rhein, Baden-Wuerttemberg, Germany, Europe, 2010
20br; **Shutterstock.com:** Everydaysunshine 67 (A), Joe Gough 67 (C), Stuart Jenner
46l, Maridav 18bl, Michaeljung 50b, Dinesh Picholiya 67 (D), Anna Shepulova 67 (E),
Szefei 67 (B); **The Kobal Collection:** No Trace Camping / Caramel Film / Fastnet
Films 9tr, Paramount 9tl, United Artists 48tr

All other images © Pearson Education